THE LEEK COOKBOOK

The
Leek
Cookbook

MARY HAMILTON

Madrona Publishers　　　　　**Seattle**

Published by
Madrona Publishers, Inc.
2116 Western Avenue
Seattle, Washington 98121

First Edition
10 9 8 7 6 5 4 3 2 1

Library of Congress Cataloging in Publication Data

Hamilton, Mary Preus.
The leek cookbook.

Includes index.
1. Cookery (Leeks)   I. Title.
TX803.L4H35   641.6′526   81-20857
ISBN 0-914842-77-3   AACR2

Drawings by Nancy Williams Nelson

To
dear George, who introduced me
to leeks,
Louise, who inspired me to write
about them,
and the many others who helped me
with this book —especially
my mother.

Contents

THE LEEK COOKBOOK

ONE

Discovering Leeks

WHAT delicious, onionlike vegetable is easily grown, resistant to pests and diseases, and can be harvested garden fresh throughout the winter? If you don't know the answer, you owe it to yourself to discover leeks.

As its botannical name suggests, *Allium porrum* is a member of the onion family, along with garlic, chives, shallots, scallions, onions and a few others. Sometimes called the gourmet onion, leeks have a flavor that is sweeter and more delicate than its close relatives. Generally, the long white stem (properly the swollen, elongated base of the leaves) is eaten, though the sharper-tasting green tops are delicious too.

Though relatively undiscovered in this country, leeks have been cultivated around the world for three or four thousand years. There continues to be some controversy about their exact origin—Switzerland, Algeria and the Eastern Mediterranean all claiming the distinction. Biblical references indicate that they were grown by several ancient civilizations of the Middle East. Numbers 11:5 records the complaints of the Israelites who wearied of manna in the Sinai wilderness in about 1200 B.C.: "We remember the fish, which we did eat in Egypt freely; the cucumbers, and the melons, and the leeks, and the onions, and the garlic...."

The Roman emperor Nero is said to have eaten leeks regularly to clear his voice, earning himself the nickname "Porrophagus"—Leek Eater. A Roman leek soup recipe from the first century A.D. appears in the soup section of this book.

According to old records, leeks were also grown in the garden of early Benedictine monasteries in Switzerland and elsewhere, including St. Gaul's, a particular favorite of Charlemagne. The *Capitulare de Villis Imperiabilis*, written by Charlemagne in the year 812 A.D., includes leeks in the list of plants to be grown in his royal gardens.

Today leeks are widely grown throughout Europe and parts of Asia. They are an indispensable element of French cuisine, so common they are called the "asparagus of the poor." A classic French work, *The Vegetable Garden* by Mme. Vilmorin-Andrieux, describes eight varieties of leeks in its 1885 English edition. Names like Large Yellow Pitou, Giant Carentan, Brabant Short Broad, and Large Rouen suggest widespread popularity; it is likely different areas in France produced their own varieties of leek. Of the Long Paris Winter Leek, Mme. Vilmorin writes, "It is the only kind which produces those fine, very long, slender Leeks, which are seen in long bundles at the Central Market in Paris...." At least three of the varieties mentioned in the book are still grown, and the firm of Vilmorin remains one of the leading seed companies of France.

Recognizing and appreciating the distinct flavor of leeks, French cooks use them imaginatively in everyday meals and haute cuisine. Leeks are commonly sold in two sizes: the smaller, more tender leeks are preferred for cooking whole; the larger ones are used in purées, soups, stews, or stuffed with a variety of fillings.

Leeks are a favorite vegetable in many other countries — an Asian variety, for example, is a staple food in Japan. It may be in the British Isles, however, that leeks are most fully appreciated. The name leek comes from the Old English word for the plant, *leac*. Centuries ago in England, the vegetable gardens were dominated by leeks to such an extent that gardeners were called "leek wards." Along with cibols (young onions) and chives, leeks were "wont to be used in Sallads to temper the coolness of other hearbes used in Salads," according to a gardening book written in the early 1600s entitled *The Countrie Farme*. To this day, there are highly competitive leek-growing contests in parts of Northern England, with considerable sums awarded to the winners. There is even a town, in Staffordshire, called Leek.

Each of the countries of Great Britain has a national emblem from the plant world. The rose was chosen for England, the shamrock for Ireland, the thistle for Scotland, and for Wales—the leek. It all came to pass, as the story goes, because of an ancient victory over the Saxons, when Welsh soldiers tucked leeks in their hats to distinguish one another from their enemies. Even now, loyal Welshmen are said to wear leeks on St. David's day in honor of the leader of their troops.

Cultivated leeks were among the vegetables brought to the New World by early immigrants from Europe. A Dutch settler, Adrian van der Donck, described the herbs grown in his garden in Yonkers, New York, in 1653: "angelica, calamus aromaticus, malva origaenum, geranium, altheae, viola, iris, indigo silvestris, coriander, leeks, wild leeks...." George Washington grew "winter onions"—probably leeks—in his kitchen garden at Mount Vernon. Such an avid gardener was Washington that he wrote, "The more I am acquainted with agricultural affairs, the better I am pleased with them; insomuch that I can no where find so great a satisfaction as in those innocent and useful pursuits." By 1800, several domestic varieties of leeks were available in the United States. Yet in spite of their early introduction, leeks have been largely overlooked in this country.

What makes leeks such a popular favorite abroad? Flavor, versatility, hardiness, and ease of growing. And now, as rising fuel costs continue to drive up the price of food, more and more Americans are shopping for regionally-grown produce in season or gardening year round—and discovering leeks.

TWO

Leeks in the Garden

NOTHING can compare with a prime quality leek fresh from the garden—the pearly white stalk shading into delicate green, then the bluish-green of the leaves—and for this you may have to grow your own. Known as the "queen of the cool weather garden," leeks thrive in all temperate regions and will withstand several degrees of frost. In many areas, they can be left in the ground to overwinter and dug for fresh eating throughout the cold months and well into spring.

Growing leeks is not complicated. They are considered by many gardeners as the best of winter vegetables. Leeks do well in most soils, though they prefer crumbly, rich loam. Like onions, they need plenty of fertilizer—well rotted manure or good compost dug into the soil is best—and abundant moisture, especially in the early stages.

Leeks are slow-growing vegetables. They require 70 to 130 days to reach maturity, depending on the variety, so choose your garden spot for them accordingly. Seeds can be planted directly in the garden as soon as the ground can be worked. Sow at a depth of ¼ inch and about a thumb's width apart, with rows about 18 inches apart. As the seedlings come up, thin them gradually to give 6 inches or so between plants. Don't toss the thinnings away; they can be used like green onions in your kitchen. Keep the seedlings moist and weeded, and that's about all it takes to produce a crop that will amply repay your labors.

For early or jumbo-sized leeks, sow the seed indoors in flats (generally February or March), 2 or 3 months before transplanting them outdoors. This procedure can save you money and ensure better spacing between plants. When the young seedlings have gained their second leaves, transfer them directly from the flats to the garden, placing them in holes made with a small dibble or trowel.

Water the plants and press the soil down around them, taking care that the roots are well spread-out and that plenty of leaf surface remains above the ground.

We transplant our seedlings twice, first to a "nursery bed," and later when they are about the thickness of a pencil (usually in mid-May), into the designated garden spot where they will remain through the following winter. Each time the leeks are transplanted, we place them deeper into the soil. This helps to make the stems long, tender, and delicate in flavor.

According to some gardening books, leeks are subject to the same pests and diseases as onions—mildew, neck rot, eelworm, and onion fly—but we haven't seen a sign of any of them. Even the slugs (a common garden pest in our area) steer clear of our leeks. In a garden where the soil is in good condition and where there is a diversity of vegetables, and crops are rotated from year to year, pests and diseases will seldom be a problem.

Autumn blanching? This is sometimes recommended to produce longer white stems. We've tried it by either setting the seedlings in trenches or pegging boards along each side of the plants. In our experience, the results didn't justify the additional work—now we plant varieties which have been bred to have extra long white stems, but we also enjoy the tender green tops. A light mulch of leaves or straw can help keep weeds down and retain moisture, but that's a matter of choice.

Leeks can be enjoyed at any stage of growth, but when the sharp frosts hit, they really come into their own. Although they stop growing, from that time on they're ready to harvest. In mild winter climates where temperatures seldom drop to below 10 degrees, Mother Nature takes care of storage—you can dig fresh, delicious leeks straight from the garden as you need them. Where winters are more severe, the plants can be heavily mulched, or moved to a root cellar or cool greenhouse and heeled into damp soil to prevent drying out.

Seed catalogs list several varieties of leeks. Broad London or American Flag (130 days) and Giant Musselburgh (90 days) are standard types that generally produce very large, stocky leeks. Burpee, Parks, and Stokes are among the seed companies which carry one or more of these varieties. Another variety, Unique (100 days), listed by Stokes, has proved to be an excellent leek with long white stems and extra hardiness. King Richard LD is offered by Johnny's Selected Seeds as "the quickest growing, tallest leek in our trials," maturing in just 75 days. An established British firm, Unwins, has the largest selection of varieties I've come across; their U.S. catalog describes 5 varieties I haven't seen listed elsewhere, including one called Marble Pillar—claimed to have stems up to 25 percent longer than any other variety given the same conditions.

We haven't come across a hybrid leek yet (nor a patented one), which means you can harvest your own supply of seeds, too. There is a certain satisfaction in planting seeds you have grown yourself, in taking part in the natural garden cycle. Beyond that, there are practical considerations that make seed saving worthwhile. By saving your own seed you become a bit more self-sufficient and less dependent on a seed company for a favorite variety that could be discontinued and lost. And if you choose parent stock with care, you may in time develop a strain of leek that is particularly well suited to your growing conditions and culinary preferences.

Parent plants can be selected in the fall or spring—check for qualities such as size, length of stalk, general plant health, hardiness, and slowness to bolt to seed. Since the process of saving seed takes several months, in springtime we move our choice plants to a special corner of the garden where they won't be in the way. If you are concerned about keeping different varieties pure, make sure that they are at least 100 feet apart when blooming to prevent cross-pollination.

If you live in an area with severe winters, mulch or hill up your parent leeks to protect them. In late spring of their second year, unharvested leeks will send up single stalks 4 to 5 feet tall, each topped with a globe of lavendar-colored flowers. By autumn, the small, angular seeds will begin to ripen and turn black. When at least one fourth of the seeds are ripe and exposed, cut the seedhead off the stalk. Hang to dry for 2 to 3 weeks until seeds can be rubbed from the heads easily. Store the seeds in an airtight container until sowing time returns again. Leek seeds remain viable for about 2 years.

You can get a head start by planting the corms that sometimes develop at the base of the plant during its second season. These little growths, which look like garlic cloves, store food energy for new plants. Dig them carefully in early spring, tucking them in about 5 inches deep, and each one should produce a fine early plant.

Some people like to eat leeks whenever they get a chance, others prefer to wait until midwinter when fresh leeks make a superb treat. If you're of the former persuasion you can, with a little planning, enjoy leeks all year round.

THREE

Cooking with Leeks: Preparation and Ingredients

ALTHOUGH leeks are as versatile as onions and delicious in their own right, most North American cookbooks give short shrift to this fine vegetable. There is really no good reason for this, since they are easy to prepare and can lend a gourmet touch to any meal. Their flavor and slightly mucilaginous quality make leeks a natural for soups—and indeed, they are an important ingredient in some of the world's classics. Leeks add something special to the flavor of appetizers, main dishes, and stews that no other member of the onion family can quite match. They also make appealing salads, used like scallions or marinated in a flavorful dressing. Nutritionally, leeks contain calcium, phosphorous, iron and vitamins A, B, and C. Half a cup contains 2 grams of protein and only 40 calories.

Leeks are available in markets from early autumn to late spring and in some parts of the country can be bought year round. They are generally sold in bunches of 2 to 6, which weigh about a pound altogether. In selecting the best quality, size is less important than freshness. Look for leeks with long white stalks and green tops free from wilting, yellowing, or bruising. Any with a hard, translucent pith has begun to go to seed and is past its prime—the center will stay hard when cooked, though the leaves are still good. Local farmers' markets or roadside produce stands often offer better, fresher vegetables than supermarkets, which usually sell fruits and vegetables that have been transported long distances.

To prepare your leeks, trim off the rootlets and the upper part of the green tops. Several inches of green will be tender enough for eating—judging the point at which the leaves become too coarse to use comes with experience, and more can be utilized than is generally thought. (In fact, many leek recipes can be made successfully using only the green tops.) Next, slit the entire green part lengthwise with a knife and wash very thoroughly, as soil has a way of working itself down the stalks.

Slice leeks in rounds, lengthwise, diagonally or in julienne strips; chop them fine or use them whole. Length or thickness of the slices will depend on the circumference of the leeks and the way you are planning to cook them. Inch-thick rounds of very large leeks, steamed or poached lightly to hold their shape, for example, work well served in the pan with a sauce, or arranged in the bottom of a quiche or jelled salad—but in other recipes, the stirring involved can break up the rounds and the resulting wide strips may not be desirable. Bite-sized diagonal slices are nice for variety. Asian cooks make attractive diamond shapes 1 to 2 inches long from small or medium-sized leeks by turning the stalks after every diagonal slice. The diamonds retain their shape and turn bright green when briefly stir-fried over high heat. Coarse chopping or cutting into julienne strips the length and width of matchsticks is fine for soups, quiches, and casseroles, while mincing is better for most green salads. Small leeks are elegant braised or marinated whole, but larger ones prepared in these ways will usually be better split in half lengthwise.

Leeks will keep for about 3 weeks if wrapped in plastic and stored in the refrigerator, though there will be some deterioration in quality, especially of the outer leaves. If possible, rootlets should be left on till the leeks are to be used. Leeks may be preserved for longer periods by freezing or drying. To freeze, slice into 1-inch rounds and steam blanch for 5 minutes. Drain, package, and place in the freezer. To dry, finely chop the leeks and spread onto trays; place in the oven at a very low heat for about 4 hours.

Every cook has definite opinions about kitchen equipment, and here are some of mine. Fine utensils and cookware add greatly to the pleasure of preparing good food. Even when used daily they will last for years, as long as they are well cared for. Good knives properly sharpened make all the difference. A set of French knives in 3 sizes, plus an Oriental-style vegetable knife, are all you need. As for pots and pans, enamel, cast-iron, glass and stainless steel are preferable to aluminum, which can leave a taste and is controversial from a health standpoint. My favorite sizes of pots are 1-quart, 2½-quart, and 10-quart stockpots. A 16-quart "superpot" comes in handy, though it's certainly not essential for any of the recipes in this book. For skillets, I like 6-inch, 10-inch, and 14-inch sizes. A couple of oven-to-table baking dishes are very useful for casseroles, and a heavy cast-iron Dutch oven with a tight fitting lid is perfect for simmering soups and stews or for braising.

A stainless steel basket steamer is a wonderful little contraption which saves both nutrients and energy. Since steam is hotter than boiling water, it cooks food faster while preventing vitamin loss. Any excess cooking water can be saved for stock. A blender is a very versatile appliance, good for making soups, sauces, purées, and even soufflés. A food mill is a non-electric alternative, though on the average a blender uses only one kilowatt hour per month.

A few words about the recipes in this book. You will find that leeks vary considerably in size—a medium specimen yields about 2 cups when sliced or chopped if the tender green tops are included—so the amount of leeks specified is just a guide. Use more or less according to your own taste.

Other proportions and ingredients may be altered as well. Substitutions can save time (meat or vegetable bouillon for stock) and lower calorie counts (evaporated milk for cream, margarine or oil for butter). Recipes have been tested with fine-ground whole wheat flour, tastier and more nutritious than white flour. Honey, a natural food, has been used instead of refined sugar when a small amount of additional sweetness is needed. The use of salt is a matter of personal preference or dietary requirements. Since I use it sparingly myself and have prepared these recipes without it, I've indicated that salt be added "to taste."

Herbs and spices can replace salt with a variety of interesting flavors. Many cooks feel that herbs are at their best when picked fresh, and it is very pleasant to grow a few plants in pots or in a kitchen garden. For winter use, herbs can be frozen in small plastic bags or dried on screens out of direct sunlight. Dried herbs, either grown at home or store-bought, are at least 3 times stronger than fresh; as a rule of thumb, a teaspoon dried herbs is the equivalent of a tablespoon fresh.

Some of the ingredients used in this book may be unfamiliar, as they originate in other countries and are only recently becoming popular throughout the United States. Quality natural soy sauce, also called *tamari* or *shoyu*, is made of soybeans brewed with water and salt. It is more expensive but far superior to the commercial soy sauce prepared from defatted soybeans processed with hydrochloric acid, flavored and colored with corn syrup and caramel, and preserved with chemicals. *Miso* is a paste made from soybeans mixed with salt and grain—usually rice or barley—and fermented. It comes in a wide range of flavors, colors, and textures. Miso can be used sparingly as a relish or spread, or as a flavor booster in sauces, soups, savories, and even desserts. *Tofu*, or soybean curd, is made by grinding soybeans soaked in water, then straining off the white soy "milk." A coagulant such as epsom salts or *nigari* (a natural sea salt) is added to separate the whey from the curds, which are then pressed into soft white blocks. Tofu stays fresh only if kept in water. It is very high in protein, and due to its bland flavor combines well with a wide variety of foods. *Mirin* is sweet rice wine made without adding sugar or other sweeteners to the fermenting rice. It is delicate in flavor and can be used instead of honey or other sweetenings in many recipes. These Oriental-style products can be found in health food stores or specialty shops, although they are also becoming available in many supermarkets.

The recipes in this book are intended as starting points, suggestions that will stimulate you to use leeks confidently, creatively, and often—in other words, to discover the pleasures of leek cookery for yourself.

FOUR

Appetizers, Spreads, and Sauces

WHAT better place to begin an introduction to the pleasures of leek cookery than with the first course of a meal? The sweet, onionlike flavor of leeks makes for distinctive appetizers, whether they are served to whet the appetite before dinner or as appealing party snacks.

For Leeks à la Grecque, baby leeks are simmered, then chilled, in an oil and vinegar marinade. Minced, uncooked leeks are combined with cheeses, nuts, herbs, and garlic in the Herbed Cheese Ball. Salinas Valley Tartlets mingle the flavors of leeks, artichoke hearts, and eggs, and are delicious warm from the oven or cooled to room temperature.

Leeks served with a good sauce make a simple but elegant appetizer or vegetable course. The flavor of lemon complements leeks particularly well, as in Blender Hollandaise Sauce, Sesame-Lemon Sauce, or simple Lemon Butter. A rich cream sauce is also excellent with leeks, as are its many variations.

Leeks à la Grecque   SERVES 6

Other vegetables such as mushrooms, celery, and green peppers are also delicious prepared in this way and combine well with the leeks.

½ cup olive oil
1½ cups water
Juice of 2 lemons
½ teaspoon dried thyme
1 bay leaf
2 sprigs parsley
¼ teaspoon celery seed
1 teaspoon fennel seeds or dried tarragon (optional)
Pinch of pepper
6 to 8 medium leeks, whole or split lengthwise

Place all ingredients except leeks in a glass or stainless steel pan. Bring to a boil, then simmer 15 minutes. Add the leeks and simmer until tender. Cool in the marinade and serve as an appetizer.

Holiday Fish Paté

SERVES 6

2 envelopes unflavored gelatin
¼ cup dry white wine
½ pound white fish fillets, such as sole, halibut, or cod
1½ cups water or clam juice
¼ cup Neufchatel or cream cheese
¼ cup plain yogurt
1 small leek or green tops of two, minced
Cucumber slices, carrot curls, radish roses

Soften the gelatin in the wine. Combine the fish and water in a saucepan and simmer for 5 minutes. Stir in softened gelatin and simmer, stirring constantly, until gelatin is dissolved. Remove from heat.

Place the chese and yogurt in a blender, add the fish mixture, and whirl until smooth. Stir in the minced leek, pour into a 1½-pint mold and chill until set or overnight. Unmold and garnish with cucumbers, carrots, and radishes before serving.

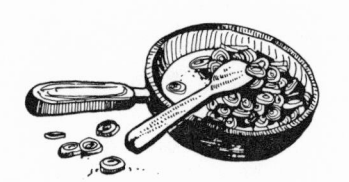

Negi Shigayaki—Japanese Leeks with Miso Sauce
SERVES 6

The authentic Japanese method of cooking this is over hot coals on a grill.

5 medium leeks, cut in 1½-inch slices or diamonds
2 tablespoons sesame or other oil
¼ cup red miso (see page 15)
1 tablespoon honey
2 tablespoons mirin (see page 15)
2 tablespoons water

Heat the oil in a heavy skillet, add the leeks and stir-fry until just tender. Make a sauce of the remaining ingredients, brush over the leeks, and broil about 10 inches from heating element until the sauce forms a glaze. Be careful not to scorch. Skewer the leeks on toothpicks and serve hot.

Salinas Valley Tartlets
SERVES 6

1 small leek, or green tops of 2, chopped fine
1 clove garlic, minced
2 tablespoons oil
5 eggs, well beaten
¾ cup fine whole wheat bread crumbs
2 tablespoons minced parsley
¼ teaspoon Tabasco sauce
½ to 1 teaspoon Worcestershire sauce
¼ teaspoon each dried oregano, basil, and thyme
Salt and pepper to taste
8 ounces sharp Cheddar cheese, grated
1 14-ounce can artichoke hearts, drained and chopped

Sauté the leeks and garlic in oil. Combine the beaten eggs with the bread crumbs, parsley, Tabasco, Worcestershire, herbs, salt and pepper. Add the sautéed leeks, cheese, and artichoke hearts. Spoon into greased miniature muffin tins (or a 9-by-12 inch baking pan) and bake 20 minutes at 325 degrees.

Herbed Cheese Ball
SERVES 10

1 pound Neufchatel or cream cheese
¼ pound aged white Cheddar, grated
3 teaspoons lemon juice or 1 teaspoon Worcestershire sauce
⅓ cup finely minced leek, including green tops
⅓ cup finely minced fresh parsley
½ teaspoon dried marjoram, thyme, or rosemary
½ teaspoon black pepper
¾ cup finely chopped almonds or walnuts

Soften the cream cheese at room temperature, then combine with all other ingredients except nuts. Shape into a ball and roll in the chopped nuts. Chill until firm and serve with crackers or Melba toast for dipping. The recipe keeps for about 2 weeks if refrigerated.

Salmon Roll
SERVES 6

¼ cup chopped leeks, including green tops
1 8-ounce package cream cheese
1 to 2 tablespoons lemon juice
1 can salmon, or 1 cup smoked salmon, flaked
Dash of Tabasco sauce
½ cup chopped almonds
½ cup chopped fresh parsley

Combine all ingredients except almonds and parsley and shape into a roll. Spread the almonds and parsley on a sheet of waxed paper and roll the salmon mixture in it until evenly covered. Chill thoroughly. Slice and serve with crackers.

Korean Meatballs   MAKES 4 DOZEN MEATBALLS

Baby meatballs in a sweet and sour sauce with the unexpected crunch of water chestnuts—delicious hot or cold as hors d'oeuvres.

Meatballs

¾ pound lean ground beef
¼ pound ground pork
¾ cup rolled oats
½ cup milk
¼ cup chopped water chestnuts
1½ teaspoons Worcestershire sauce
1 medium leek, chopped fine
1 clove garlic, minced
2 to 3 drops Tabasco sauce
2 tablespoons butter

Combine all ingredients except butter and shape into 4 dozen small balls. Melt the butter in a heavy frying pan and brown the meatballs. Pour off any grease, then add Sweet and Sour Sauce (below), cover, and simmer 30 minutes. Place a toothpick in each meatball before serving.

Sweet and Sour Sauce

¾ to 1 cup honey
¾ cup cider vinegar
¾ cup water
1 teaspoon paprika
1 tablespoon soy sauce
2 teaspoons cornstarch
1 tablespoon water

Combine the honey, vinegar, water, paprika, and soy sauce in a saucepan and cook for 5 minutes. Blend the cornstarch with water and add to saucepan. Cook over a medium heat, stirring constantly, until slightly thickened.

Stuffed Mushroom Caps

SERVES 6

1 large leek, sliced in ½-inch rounds
12 very large fresh mushrooms
½ to 1 pound ground hot Italian sausage
½ cup grated Parmesan cheese

Steam the leek rounds until tender, taking care not to break them up when handling. Drain. Any extra leek may be set aside for other use.

Wipe the mushrooms clean and remove the stems. Stuff each mushroom cap with 1 or 2 leek rounds, cover with about 1 tablespoon of sausage, then sprinkle with the Parmesan cheese. Set the mushrooms on a baking sheet and broil for about 5 minutes. Serve hot.

Guacamole

MAKES 3½ CUPS

2 large ripe avocados, mashed
¼ cup minced leek
1 to 2 teaspoons minced fresh parsley
2 tablespoons lemon juice, more to taste
1 large tomato, peeled and diced
Pinch of cayenne pepper
Salt to taste

Combine all ingredients, squeezing a little extra lemon juice over the top to preserve color if the guacamole is not to be used promptly. This is delicious as a dip, spread, or, thinned with a little water or tomato juice, salad dressing.

Mock Sour Cream

MAKES 1½ CUPS

1 cup cottage cheese
¼ cup yogurt
2 tablespoons mayonnaise
2 tablespoons oil
2 tablespoons tarragon vinegar
1 tablespoon minced fresh or 1 to 2 teaspoons dried tarragon
Salt and pepper to taste

Combine all ingredients in a blender until smooth, adding a little milk or water to thin if necessary. More nutritious and less fattening than ordinary sour cream, this makes a fine accompaniment for steamed leeks.

Green Sauce

MAKES 2½ CUPS

1 medium leek, including green top, coarsely chopped
2 cloves garlic, mashed
¼ cup olive oil
1½ cups stock or water
¼ head romaine lettuce, coarsely chopped
2 stalks celery, chopped
1 bunch parsley, coarsely chopped
3 tablespoons fresh basil, chopped
1 teaspoon fresh mint or rosemary
Salt and pepper to taste
2 tablespoons lemon juice
⅓ cup raw sunflower seeds (optional)

Sauté the leek and garlic in oil. Add the stock, romaine, celery, herbs, salt and pepper. Cover and simmer 10 minutes, add the sunflower seeds, then purée in a blender. Stir in the lemon juice and serve hot or cold over leeks, fresh vegetables, or pasta. This sauce can also be frozen—a little lemon juice squeezed over the top will prevent darkening during thawing.

Cucumber Sauce
MAKES 2 CUPS

½ cup sour cream
½ cup mayonnaise
1 tablespoon minced leek
1 tablespoon finely chopped dill pickle or fresh dill weed
1 large cucumber, peeled and chopped
1 teaspoon capers (optional)

Combine the sour cream, mayonnaise, leek, and dill. Add the cucumber and capers and chill. Serve with salmon or other fish. This is also delicious as a salad dressing, spooned over a platter of lettuce, tomato wedges, and whole green beans steamed tender-crisp.

Cream Sauce
MAKES 1 CUP

2 tablespoons butter or corn oil
2 tablespoons fine-ground whole wheat flour
1 cup whole milk or light cream
Salt and pepper to taste

Melt the butter in a saucepan over a low heat. Stir in the flour and blend well, cooking until the flour just begins to brown. Add the milk slowly, stirring constantly to avoid lumps. Continue cooking over a low heat until the sauce begins to thicken and bubble. Season with salt and pepper.

This version of a cream sauce freezes successfully if the butter and flour are thoroughly combined before milk is added. I often double the recipe and put half in the freezer for later use.

VARIATIONS

Cheese Sauce

Follow directions for Cream Sauce, adding 1 teaspoon dry mustard with the flour. When the sauce has thickened, stir in ¾ cup Cheddar or Swiss cheese, or a combination of either with Parmesan. Makes 1½ cups.

Leek Cream Sauce

Follow directions for Cream Sauce, adding ¼ cup finely chopped leek to the melted butter and cooking gently for 3 minutes before adding the flour. Makes 1 cup.

Curry Cream Sauce

Season basic Cream Sauce with 1 to 2 teaspoons curry powder. Makes 1 cup.

Miso Cream Sauce

Add 2 to 4 teaspoons red or brown miso (see page 15) as the last ingredient, first mixing the miso with a little sauce to make a smooth paste. Warm through before serving. Makes 1 cup.

Blender Hollandaise Sauce   MAKES 1 CUP

¾ cup butter
3 egg yolks
3 tablespoons lemon juice
Salt and white pepper to taste

Melt the butter over a low heat. Combine remaining ingredients in a blender and process for a few seconds to mix well. Slowly pour the hot butter into the blender, drop by drop at first and then in a thin stream, continuing to blend until smooth.

For variety, add 1 to 2 tablespoons coarsely chopped fresh herbs, such as tarragon, parsley, sweet basil, or savory before blending in the butter.

Sesame-Lemon Sauce
MAKES 1 CUP

3 egg yolks
1 whole egg
Juice of 1 large lemon
1 cup hot stock or bouillon
2 tablespoons toasted sesame seeds

Beat the egg yolks and whole egg until thick and lemon-colored. Gradually add the lemon juice, then the stock, beating constantly. If the sauce does not thicken enough, heat it over simmering water, stirring continually until thick. Add the sesame seeds last, or sprinkle on top as a garnish.

Lemon Butter
MAKES ½ CUP

½ cup butter, softened at room temperature
2 tablespoons lemon juice

Cream the butter until fluffy, and add the lemon juice. Serve over hot steamed leeks.

Leek and Herb Butter

MAKES 1 CUP

1 cup butter, softened at room temperature
½ cup coarsely chopped leeks, including green tops
¼ cup parsley sprigs, packed down
1 teaspoon celery seed
¼ teaspoon crushed dried marjoram or basil
¼ teaspoon crushed dried thyme
1 clove garlic, mashed
Pinch of black pepper
1 to 2 tablespoons lemon juice

Place all ingredients in a blender and process until well mixed. Serve over leeks or other vegetables, add a dab to soups or sauces, or spread on sandwiches. Herb butter can be stored in the refrigerator for weeks, or frozen for later use.

FIVE

Soups

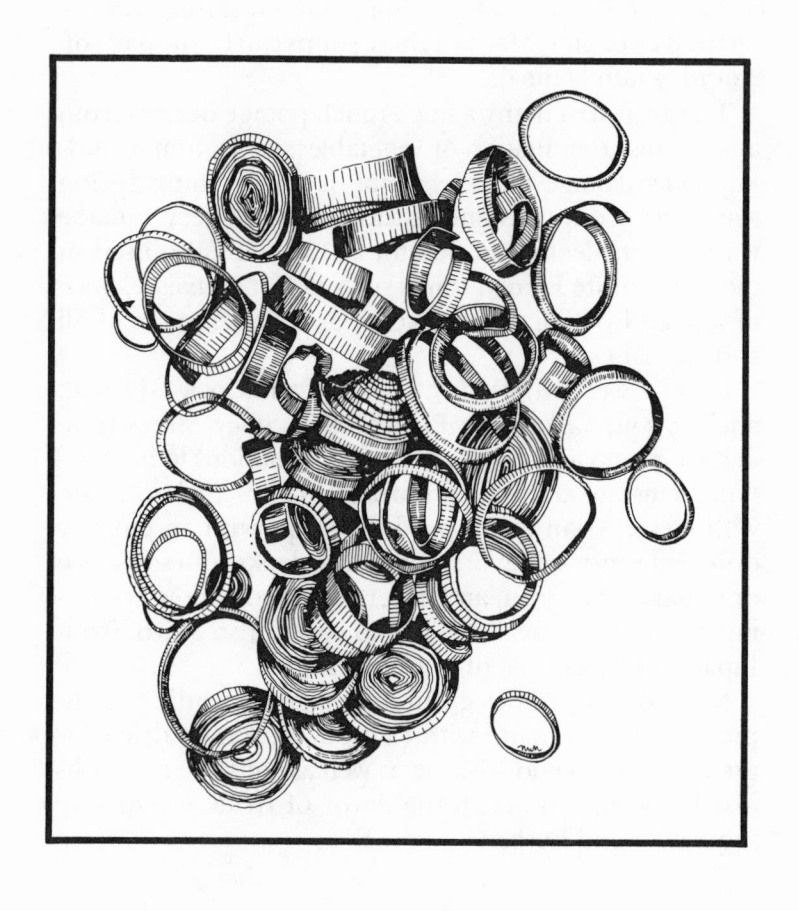

LEEK and Potato Soup, a hearty, delicious, and adaptable soup, is the one leek recipe that has earned a place in most general North American cookbooks. Yet cooks around the world have known for centuries that the subtle sweetness of leeks can harmonize a diversity of flavors into a savory unity, making leeks an important ingredient in a wide variety of soups. Roman Leek Soup, dating back hundreds of years, is an early example; more modern ones range from savory Vegetable Stock to creamy Mushroom Leek Soup, chilled Vichyssoise for a summer's evening or German Oxtail Soup for satisfying winter-whetted appetites. Many of these soups can be the basis of everyday family meals.

The appeal of many a fine French potage derives from a felicitous combination of vegetables, very often including leeks. Potage Ste. Germaine is a refreshing spring soup with fresh peas and lettuce; Potage Crécy is made with carrots, leeks and potatoes. Leeks are also used in more elaborate French soups such as Bouillabaisse, once described by William Thackeray as a "hotchpotch of all sorts of fishes."

Leeks are essential in Scotch Broth and Cock-a-Leekie, ancient soups from the British Isles. Spicy Minestrone and Cioppino and among Italy's contributions to international cuisine, and they are best, of course, when made with leeks. Asian cooks produce soups with an entirely different range of flavors, combining leeks with soy sauce or tamari, miso, tofu, and other ingredients now becoming more readily available in the West. Miso Shiro, from Japan, is an example of one such soup.

Many of the recipes given here take very little time to prepare. Soups made with canned, frozen or dried ingredients can be nourishing as well as convenient. Nothing, however, can match the flavor of fresh, top-quality vegetables and herbs.

Roman Leek Soup

This recipe was recorded by an Englishman named Langham in 1579.

"Nature to restore, eat of this Soupe first & last (morning and evening): Marrow Bones with the flesh, Leekes, Pepper, Ginger, Cinnamon & Nutmeg."

Vegetable Stock   SERVES 6 TO 8

Good by itself, or as a base for soups, stews, and sauces.

1 quart water
1 quart tomato juice
3 medium carrots, sliced
1 large celeriac (if available), diced
2 medium potatoes, diced
1 onion, chopped
3 medium leeks, sliced in 1-inch pieces
2 whole bay leaves
½ cup finely chopped parsley
½ teaspoon dried rosemary, or 1 sprig fresh
½ teaspoon celery seed
Salt, pepper, and cayenne pepper to taste
2 tablespoons butter (optional)

Place the liquids in a soup kettle and add vegetables in the order given, simmering for about 5 minutes between additions. For use as a stock, stir in the seasonings and simmer for 45 to 60 minutes, until the vegetables are soft. Strain the liquid and reserve.

When serving as a soup, simmer only until the vegetables are tender, about 30 minutes, and do not remove them from the broth. Just before serving, stir in the butter. For a soup that's a meal in itself, try adding brown rice, cooked beans, or diced tofu.

Leek and Potato Soup
SERVES 8

This is a version of a favorite soup that is prepared in many forms around the world. Several variations follow.

4 medium potatos, diced
2 cups cold water
4 large leeks, including some green tops, sliced fine
1 large onion, chopped
2 tablespoons butter or oil
3 cups milk
Dash of cayenne pepper
Salt and pepper to taste
2 egg yolks, lightly beaten (optional)
2 tablespoons minced fresh parsley
1 cup cream

Place the potatoes in a 6-quart pot, add water and cook 10 minutes or until nearly tender. Sauté the leeks and onion in butter or oil until golden. Add to potatoes and stir in the milk and seasonings. Simmer until the vegetables are cooked and flavors are blended, about 15 minutes. If desired, thicken with egg yolks, first beaten with a cup of soup liquid. Add the parsley and heat almost to boiling, stirring often. Enrich the soup with the cream and serve piping hot.

VARIATIONS

Use the quantities given in the basic recipe.

Clam Chowder with Leeks

Fry ¼ pound lean bacon in soup kettle. Add the onion, then leeks, then potatoes, sautéing briefly between each addition. Omit the butter and cream and add two cans or 1 pound fresh, shucked clams with the seasonings and milk.

Crab Chowder with Leeks

Proceed as for Clam Chowder but omit the bacon and add 1 cup crabmeat, flaked, and ¼ cup sherry just before serving.

Mulligatawny Soup

Heat the oil or butter in soup kettle and stir in 1 tablespoon curry powder. Add and sauté the onion, potatoes, leeks, 1 grated carrot, and 1 chopped apple. Omit the parsley and replace the milk and cream with chicken stock.

Vegetable Cream Soup

Follow the basic recipe, adding chopped broccoli, green beans, cauliflower, carrots, celery, or other vegetables with the seasonings and milk.

Watercress Soup

Add 1 cup fresh watercress, chopped, then purée soup in a blender of food mill. Garnish with finely chopped watercress and hard-boiled egg. Serve hot or cold.

Cream of Leek Soup

Omit potatoes and use 1 additional leek.

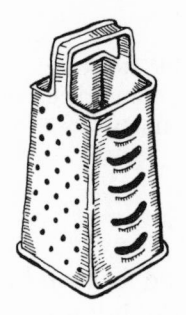

Porrosalda

A Basque variation of Leek and Potato Soup made without milk or cream.

5 slices bacon
5 tablespoons butter or oil
5 medium leeks, sliced in 1-inch rounds
5 large potatoes, diced
5 stalks celery, sliced
1 large clove garlic, minced
2 tablespoons whole wheat flour
4 quarts stock or bouillon
1 bay leaf
Pepper to taste
2 tablespoons minced parsley

Fry the bacon in a large stockpot until crisp. Remove from pan, drain, and crumble. Set aside.

Add butter or oil to bacon grease and heat. Sauté the vegetables and garlic in fat until soft. Sprinkle with the flour and stir thoroughly until browned. Add the stock, pepper, bay leaf, and cooked bacon. Simmer for 25 minutes and sprinkle with the parsley just before serving.

Vichyssoise

3 large leeks, white part only, chopped fine
4 tablespoons butter or oil
1 small onion, chopped fine
4 cups chicken or vegetable stock
3 medium potatoes, peeled and diced or sliced fine
2 tablespoons chopped parsley
Salt and pepper to taste
1 cup heavy cream
Minced chives, dill or parsley

In a stockpot, melt the leeks in butter or oil. Add the onion and sauté until soft, but not brown. Add the stock, potatoes, parsley, and seasonings. Simmer until tender, about 25 minutes. Remove from heat and purée in a blender or food mill. Stir in the cream and chill for at least 2 hours. Serve in chilled soup bowls, garnished with the minced herbs.

Potage Crécy

SERVES 6 TO 8

3 large leeks, white parts only
8 large carrots
2 stalks celery
6 to 8 cups chicken or vegetable stock
1 large bay leaf
¼ cup fresh chervil or parsley
Salt and pepper to taste
½ cup cream
2 tablespoons butter (optional)

Slice the leeks, carrots, and celery stalks thin. Combine with 2 cups of the stock in a large, heavy stockpot, adding the bay leaf and chervil or parsley. Bring to a boil and simmer until tender. Transfer the entire mixture to a bowl and ladle ⅓ of the vegetables into a blender, adding more stock as necessary to purée. Repeat until all vegetables are puréed and return them to the stockpot, along with any remaining stock. Add salt and pepper to taste.

Continue to cook until the soup is heated through. Lower heat and slowly stir in the cream. Before serving, swirl in the butter.

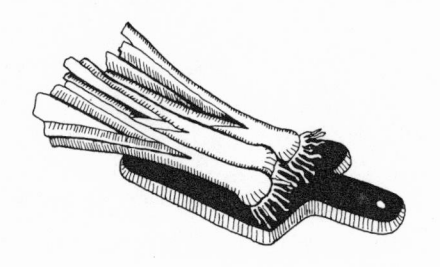

Potage Ste. Germaine
SERVES 6

2 medium leeks, sliced thin
¼ cup oil
1 to 1½ pounds fresh spinach, washed and chopped
1¼ pound peas, fresh or frozen
1 small head Bibb lettuce, coarsely shredded
4 cups chicken or vegetable stock
¼ cup honey
2 teaspoons minced fresh chervil (or parsley)
Salt and pepper to taste

Sauté the leeks gently in oil until tender. In a heavy stockpot, cook the peas, spinach, and lettuce in the stock until soft, then purée in a blender until smooth. Return the puréed vegetables to the pot, and add the sautéed leeks, honey, chervil or parsley, and seasonings. Serve hot with a sprinkling of minced chervil on each soup bowl.

Potage Trois Amies
SERVES 6

2 tablespoons butter
2 large leeks, thinly sliced
4 fresh tomatoes, or 2 cups canned, peeled and coarsely
       chopped
4 large potatoes, peeled and diced
Salt to taste
1 teaspoon honey
2½ cups cold water
¼ cup cream
3 tablespoons minced fresh chervil or parsley

Melt the butter in a heavy saucepan, add the leeks and cook gently until soft and translucent. Stir in the tomatoes and simmer for about 5 minutes. Add the potatoes, salt, and honey, cover with water, and bring to a boil. Reduce heat and simmer for 25 minutes.

Remove from heat and put through a blender or food

mill. Return to the saucepan, and heat through. Just before serving, stir in the cream and sprinkle with the chervil or parsley.

Bouillabaisse
SERVES 8

A version of the soup from the south of France. For a simpler soup that is delicious but less deluxe, omit the shellfish.

¼ cup olive oil
2 large leeks, julienned or coarsely chopped
1 onion, chopped
1 stalk celery, chopped
3 cloves garlic, pressed
4 tomatoes, or 2 cups canned, peeled and coarsely chopped
2 bay leaves
½ cup minced fresh parsley
½ teaspoon saffron
½ teaspoon dried thyme
½ teaspoon dried basil
4 cups fish stock, canned clam juice, or water
3 to 4 pounds thick fillets of firm fish such as red snapper, halibut, or black cod, cut in 2-inch chunks
2 dozen clams or mussels in the shell, well scrubbed
1 to 2 cups shelled oysters
1 cup cooked and cleaned shrimp or crab
Juice of 1 lemon

Heat the olive oil in a large stockpot and sauté the leek, onion, celery, and garlic until golden. Add the tomatoes, bay leaves, ¼ cup of the parsley, saffron, thyme, basil, and stock. Simmer 20 minutes. Add the fish fillets and simmer for 5 to 8 minutes or until they begin to flake. Add clams or mussels, oysters, and shrimp or crab and simmer until the shells open, about 5 minutes. Stir in lemon juice and sprinkle with remaining parsley. Ladle into bowls and serve with crusty French bread for eating and dunking.

Scotch Broth

SERVES 8 TO 10

3 pounds lamb bones*
Cold water to cover, about 3 quarts
½ cup barley
2 whole allspice
2 medium carrots, diced
¾ cup diced rutabaga or turnip
2 stalks celery, diced
1 onion, diced
2 medium leeks, coarsely chopped
3 tablespoons butter or oil
Salt and pepper to taste
1 sprig fresh thyme, or ½ teaspoon dried
¼ cup chopped fresh parsley

Cover the lamb bones with cold water in a large stockpot, add the barley and allspice, and bring rapidly to a boil. Simmer about 2 hours. Remove the bones, cool the broth, and skim off excess fat.

Prepare the vegetables and sauté in butter or oil until nearly tender. Combine with the lamb broth, then add the salt, pepper, and thyme, and simmer 25 minutes. Add the parsley just before serving or sprinkle over soup in serving bowls.

*Use a bone from a large leg or shoulder of lamb roast, or bony cuts like neck or flank.

Cock-a-Leekie Soup

1 3-pound stewing chicken
3 quarts cold water
2 whole cloves
½ cup raw brown rice
6 medium leeks, coarsely chopped
10 dried prunes, pitted
10 dried apricot halves
½ teaspoon black pepper
¼ cup chopped parsley
Salt to taste

Place the chicken, water and cloves in a large stockpot or Dutch oven and bring slowly to a boil. Simmer for 1 hour, then add the rice, leeks, dried fruit, and black pepper. Continue to simmer until the chicken is tender, about 45 minutes. Skim off excess fat. Remove the chicken, bone it and cut in pieces, then return to the soup with the chopped parsley. Salt to taste and heat thoroughly before serving.

Minestrone

3 medium or 2 large leeks
1 small onion
3 stalks celery
2 medium carrots
¼ cup parsley
¼ cup olive oil
6 cups tomato juice
3 large fresh tomatoes, or 2 cups canned, peeled and coarsely
    chopped
1 to 2 cloves garlic, pressed
1 bay leaf
1 teaspoon dried or 1 sprig fresh rosemary
2 teaspoons dried basil
1 teaspoon celery seed
Salt and pepper to taste

3 cups mixed raw vegetables, chopped (such as zucchini, green
      beans, cabbage, mushrooms, green peppers)
2 cups cooked white beans
1 cup raw whole wheat macaroni or other small pasta
¾ cup grated Parmesan or Romano cheese

Chop the first 5 ingredients together on a board, then
cook slowly in olive oil in a large stockpot until tender.
Add the tomato juice, tomatoes, and seasonings and
simmer 20 minutes. Stir in the mixed vegetables, white
beans, and pasta. Simmer another 20 minutes. Bring to a
boil and serve hot, garnished with the grated cheese.

Cioppino   SERVES 8 TO 10

3 medium leeks, coarsely chopped
2 large cloves garlic, minced or pressed
½ green pepper, chopped
1 cup fresh mushrooms, sliced
¼ cup olive oil
8 large fresh tomatoes, or 6 cups canned, peeled and coarsely
      chopped
1 cup tomato purée
1 teaspoon oregano
1 tablespoon chili powder
¼ cup minced fresh parsley
Clam juice or water
2 pounds red snapper or black bass fillets, cut in 2-inch chunks
1 cup shelled oysters
Shrimp, mussels, clams, scallops, or crab as desired
Dash of vermouth or white wine

Sauté the garlic, leeks, green pepper, and mushrooms
in olive oil in a stockpot or Dutch oven. Add the tomatoes,
tomato purée, oregano, chili powder, and parsley. (Celery, zucchini, carrots or other vegetables may be added
for variety.) Cover and simmer 20 to 30 minutes, until
vegetables are tender. Thin with clam juice or water if
necessary.

Add the fish fillets and simmer 5 to 8 minutes until they begin to flake. Add the shellfish and simmer another 5 minutes, till shells open. Stir in the vermouth or wine and serve in large soup bowls with French bread and salad.

German Oxtail Soup

SERVES 6

3 medium leeks, sliced in 1½-inch chunks
3 tablespoons oil
3 pounds oxtails, cut in 1-inch pieces
2 cups dry red wine
2 cups beef broth
1 6-ounce can tomato paste
3 carrots, chopped
1 small potato, diced
1 teaspoon honey
Salt and pepper to taste

In a large frying pan, sauté leeks in 2 tablespoons of the oil until soft. Transfer to a stockpot. Add the remaining oil to the frying pan and brown the meat, a few pieces at a time, adding to soup pot as you go. When all of the meat is browned, pour the wine into the frying pan and bring to a boil, scraping free any bits of meat from the bottom of the pan.

Add the wine and remaining ingredients to the stockpot. Cover and simmer about 2 to 3 hours, stirring occasionally, until the meat is very tender and the broth is thick. Serve piping hot.

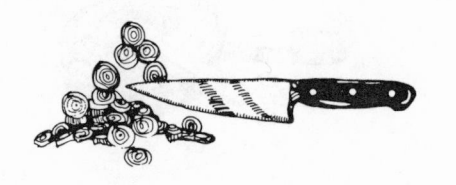

Portugese Bean Soup

SERVES 6 TO 8

Thick and spicy, this soup is almost a meal in itself.

½ pound dried kidney or pinto beans
1 large ham hock
2 quarts water
¾ pound Portugese sausage, if available, or Polish sausage ring
4 fresh tomatoes, or 2 cups canned, peeled and coarsely
        chopped
1 to 2 tablespoons chili powder
Dash of Tabasco sauce
2 cloves garlic, pressed
1 bay leaf
3 medium leeks, cut in 1½-inch pieces
3 large carrots, thickly sliced
3 potatoes, cut in chunks

Soak the dried beans in enough cold water to cover overnight. Rinse and drain.

Combine the ham hock and beans with the water in a Dutch oven or large stockpot. Bring to a boil, then simmer until tender. Remove meat from bone and return to pot, discarding bone.

Slice and add the Portugese sausage, or if Polish sausage is substituted, boil separately, drain, and slice before adding to soup. Stir in the tomatoes, add the spices and remaining vegetables, and continue to cook until the vegetables are tender. Serve hot.

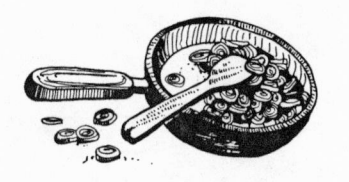

Miso Shiro

Endless variations of Miso Shiro are served for breakfast in Japan.

6 cups dashi* or water
1 large leek, cut in julienne strips
1 pound tofu, cut in ½-inch cubes (see page 15)
1 cup bean sprouts or grated carrot
½ cup red or yellow miso (see page 15)
Red pepper flakes
1 tablespoon leek slivers

Bring the dashi or water to a boil in a stockpot, add the leek and return to boiling. Stir in the tofu and the bean sprouts or carrots and simmer for 1 to 2 minutes. Blend the miso with some of the soup until it forms a smooth paste, and add to remaining soup. Return to a boil. Serve hot, garnishing each bowl with red pepper flakes and leek slivers.

*Dashi is a type of soup stock available in fresh or powdered form in health food or specialty shops.

Vietnamese Sparerib Soup (Canh Sườn)

Surprisingly, leeks are grown in the highlands of Vietnam, where the climate is similar to that of the farming valleys of California.

1 pound spareribs, cut up
6 cups cold water
2 medium potatoes, chopped
1 medium carrot, sliced
2 medium leeks, including green tops, sliced in 1-inch rounds
1 packet won ton soup flavoring mix*

Cover the spareribs with water in a stockpot and cook until tender, about ½ hour. Add the potatoes and carrot and simmer 15 to 20 minutes. Add the leeks and seasoning and simmer briefly, about 5 minutes, until the leeks are barely tender and still bright green. Serve at once.

*Won ton soup mix is available in Oriental food shops. It is possible to substitute, instead, ¼ to ½ cup red miso (see page 15). Blend the miso with a little soup stock and stir in after the leeks have been added to soup.

Fish Chowder   SERVES 6

2 pounds cod or haddock fillets
2 cups cold water
2 large potatoes, cut in ½-inch cubes
½ pound bacon
2 medium leeks, sliced in 1-inch diagonals
3 cups milk
2 tablespoons butter
Salt and pepper to taste

Place the fish fillets and water in a stockpot and simmer until the fish begins to fall apart. Remove the fish from water and flake with a fork. Add the potatoes to fish stock in pot and cook until tender.

Fry the bacon in a separate pan until crisp, remove, and drain on paper towels. Sauté the leeks lightly in the bacon grease. Crumble the bacon into soup, add the leeks and fish, then the milk, butter and seasonings. Simmer for about 10 minutes and serve hot.

Leek and Corn Chowder   SERVES 4 TO 6

2 tablespoons butter
1 large leek, julienned
2 cups fresh corn, scraped from cob, or 1 can creamed
3 cups milk
1 cup cream (if using fresh corn)
¼ teaspoon nutmeg or black pepper
Salt to taste

Melt the butter in a soup kettle. Add the leeks and cook slowly until soft but not brown. Stir in the corn, milk, cream, and seasonings. Heat nearly to a boil, and serve immediately.

Winter Vegetable Chowder   SERVES 8 TO 10

Perfect for a stick-to-the-ribs winter meal.

¼ cup oil
1 large onion, chopped
4 medium carrots, sliced
2 stalks celery with tops, chopped
3 large leeks, sliced in 1-inch rounds
3 medium potatoes, diced
6 Jerusalem artichokes, scrubbed and chopped
1 parsnip, diced
2 cups water
3 to 4 cups milk
2 tablespoons whole wheat flour
¼ cup minced parsley
Salt and pepper to taste
6 thin slices French bread, lightly toasted
1 cup grated Swiss or Gruyère cheese

Heat the oil in a large soup kettle. Add the onion, then the carrots, then the celery and leeks, sautéing each until tender. Add remaining vegetables and enough water to steam them tender.

Shake the milk and flour in a jar, then stir into the pot. Simmer, stirring frequently, until the soup thickens. Ladle into soup bowls and float a slice of French bread on top of each. Sprinkle with grated cheese and bake for 10 minutes in a 350-degree oven until the cheese is melted. Serve immediately.

Dorothy's Asparagus and Leek Soup
SERVES 4 TO 6

Invented by my wonderful next-door neighbor, Dorothy Simons.

1 pound fresh or frozen asparagus
1 medium leek, coarsely chopped
2 tablespoons cornstarch
2½ cups milk
Salt and pepper to taste

Steam the asparagus until tender, then purée in a blender or food mill. For this recipe, you can use the tough lower ends of asparagus stalks—if doing so, start with more than a pound and use a food mill. There should be about 2 cups of purée.

In a stockpot, sauté the leek in butter. Dissolve the cornstarch in ½ cup cold milk and add to the pot. Stir in the asparagus purée, and cook gently, stirring constantly until thickened. Add the remaining milk and bring almost to a boil. Remove from heat and season to taste. Serve hot, or chill thoroughly and serve cold.

Leek and Lima Cream Soup   SERVES 6 TO 8

1 cup dried lima beans
6 cups cold water
1 medium leek, thinly sliced
1 medium carrot, chopped
¼ cup chopped green pepper
2 tablespoons butter or oil
Salt and pepper to taste
½ teaspoon dried savory
2 tablespoons fine whole wheat flour
½ cup cream or whole milk
2 tablespoons butter (optional)
Paprika

Wash the beans and place in a large stockpot. Add the water and cook until very soft, about two hours.

Prepare the vegetables and sauté in butter until tender. Add the vegetables to beans and stir in the seasonings. Sprinkle the flour on top, stirring briskly to avoid lumps. Simmer 10 minutes, stirring occasionally, then whirl in a blender or purée in a food mill until smooth.

Return the soup to the pot, heat almost to boiling. Stir in the cream, and the butter if used, and serve at once, garnishing each bowl with paprika.

Mushroom Leek Soup   SERVES 4 TO 6

2 medium leeks, thinly sliced
2 tablespoons butter or oil
2 cups sliced mushrooms
3 cups milk
2 tablespoons whole wheat flour
¼ teaspoon nutmeg
½ cup cream
1 tablespoon butter
2 tablespoons sherry

Melt the leeks in the butter or oil in a stockpot. Add the mushrooms and sauté lightly. Stir in 2½ cups of the milk. Combine remaining milk with the flour and the nutmeg in a jar with a tight lid, and shake well. Add to soup, and mix thoroughly. Simmer 20 minutes, stirring occasionally. Just before serving, swirl in the cream, butter, and sherry.

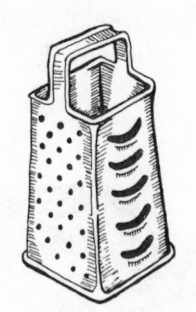

SIX

Vegetables and Side Dishes

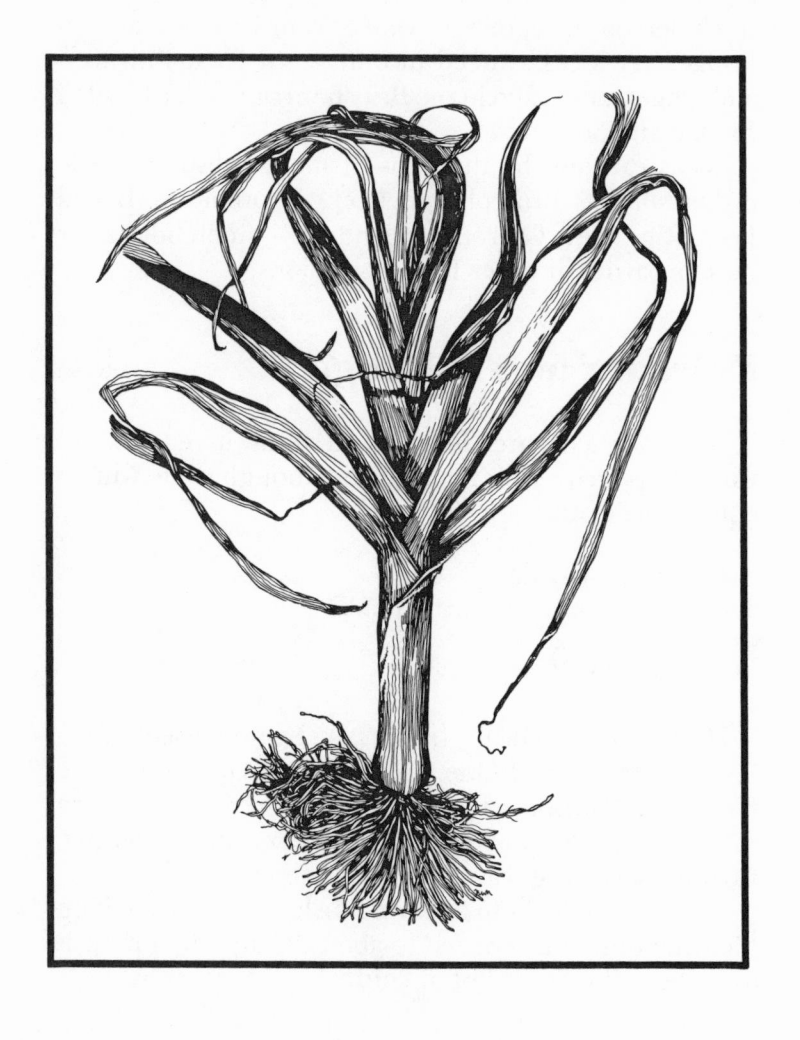

LEEKS are delicious as a vegetable in their own right, and some of the best ways to prepare them are the simplest. Though they go well with many other foods, their delicate flavor is perhaps best appreciated when they are served alone. Leeks are elegant steamed and topped with plain or herb butter, cheese, a squeeze of lemon juice, or a good sauce. They are excellent braised or poached in stock, lemon juice, or red wine—as in Poireaux au Vin Rouge. Try leeks sautéed in butter, stir-fried with tofu and ginger, or cooked in the British version of hash called Bubble and Squeak.

Leeks can also be the basis of more substantial side dishes such as Broccoli and Leeks Supreme or Baked Leek Ring with Carrots Hollandaise—fine choices for dinner parties or other festive occasions.

Poireaux au Vin Rouge   SERVES 4

In France, leeks are often cooked simply in red or white wine. This recipe calls for red wine, though white wine is equally delicious.

2 tablespoons olive oil
3 medium leeks, cut in 3-inch chunks
Salt to taste
1 cup dry red wine

Heat the oil in a heavy frying pan. Sauté the leeks for a few minutes on each side. Sprinkle with salt and remove from heat. Pour the wine over the leeks, cover and return to heat. Simmer for about 10 minutes or until just tender, turning once. Test with a fork for doneness.

Transfer the leeks to a serving dish. Continue cooking the wine until it is reduced to about ½ cup, then pour it over the leeks. Serve hot or cold.

Braised Leeks With Celery and Lettuce
SERVES 6

Leeks can also be braised solo in bouillon or wine, but this stock with the French-inspired addition of celery stalks and lettuce makes a pleasant change.

2 tablespoons butter or oil
8 stalks celery
1 large carrot, sliced
1 onion, sliced
2 tablespoons minced fresh parsley
¼ teaspoon dried thyme
4 medium leeks, whole or split lengthwise
Salt and pepper to taste
½ teaspoon paprika
2 cups coffee or cereal beverage
3 small heads Bibb or Boston lettuce, halved

Heat the butter or oil in a large heavy skillet, preferably a cast-iron one. Chop 2 stalks of celery and add to the skillet along with the carrots, onion, parsley, and thyme. Sauté gently until almost browned.

Arrange the leeks and remaining celery stalks over the vegetable mixture. Season with salt, pepper, and paprika, then pour the coffee or cereal beverage over all. Boil 5 minutes uncovered, then cover and simmer until the leeks and celery are tender, about 15 minutes.

Lay the lettuce over the leeks and celery, then simmer, covered, for 10 minutes longer, basting occasionally. Transfer to a serving dish and serve hot.

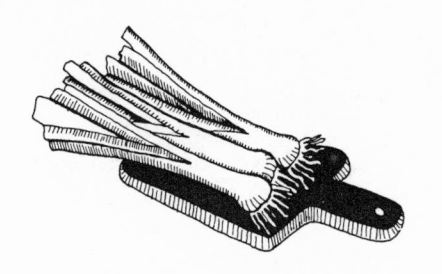

Baked Leek Ring with Carrots Hollandaise

4 large leeks, cut in 1-inch diagonals
1 cup Cream Sauce (see page 25)
2 tablespoons Dijon mustard
2 tablespoons bleu cheese, crumbled, or 1 3-ounce package
     cream cheese
Salt, pepper, and cayenne pepper to taste
1 cup whole wheat bread crumbs
3 eggs, separated
2 to 3 cups baby carrots, cooked
1 cup Blender Hollandaise Sauce (see page 26)

Steam the leeks until tender, and drain. Combine with the Cream Sauce, mustard, cheese, seasonings, bread crumbs, and egg yolks. Beat the egg whites until stiff, then fold gently into the mixture. Turn into a greased 2-quart ring mold, set in a pan of hot water, and bake for 25 minutes at 325 degrees.

Turn out of the mold onto a serving platter. Fill the center with hot, cooked carrots and glaze with Blender Hollandaise Sauce. Serve immediately.

Rumanian Leeks

2 medium or large leeks, sliced in 1-inch pieces
3 large tomatoes, peeled and chopped
½ cup black olives, or green olives with pimientos
Juice of 1 lemon

Simmer the leeks with the tomatoes in a covered saucepan until tender, adding a little water if necessary. Soak the olives in hot water for 10 minutes to remove salt, and drain. Transfer the leeks and tomatoes to serving dish and sprinkle with the olives. Squeeze the lemon over all and serve warm or cold.

Quick Leeks au Gratin SERVES 6

Delicious and simple.

6 medium leeks
2 cups grated Cheddar, Swiss or Gruyère cheese

Slice the leeks lengthwise or chop into bite-size rounds. Steam until tender but not mushy, arrange in a shallow baking dish, and sprinkle with the grated cheese. Pop under broiler until the cheese melts.

Broccoli and Leeks Supreme SERVES 6 TO 8

1 pound fresh broccoli
4 medium leeks, sliced in 1-inch pieces
2 tablespoons butter
4 tablespoons finely ground whole wheat flour
1 cup milk
3 ounces cream cheese, softened
Salt and pepper to taste
½ to 1 cup grated Cheddar or Gruyère cheese
1 cup buttered bread crumbs

Cut the broccoli into 1-inch pieces and cook until just tender. Steam the leeks separately and drain.

Melt the butter in a medium saucepan, stir in the flour and cook lightly. Stir in the milk and continue to cook until smooth and bubbly. Season, reduce heat, and blend in the cream cheese.

Place the steamed vegetables in a 1½-quart casserole. Pour the sauce over it and mix lightly. Top with the grated cheese and bake, covered, at 350 degrees for 30 minutes. Sprinkle the bread crumbs over the top and bake uncovered until lightly browned.

This recipe is particularly good for a make-ahead dish. Just cover the casserole and chill until you are ready to bake.

Stir-Fried Leeks with Tofu   SERVES 4

There are many variations to this basic recipe. Try adding bean sprouts, sliced mushrooms, green peppers, Jerusalem artichokes, or any of your favorite vegetables.

2 tablespoons oil
1 clove garlic, minced
3 medium leeks, sliced in 1-inch diamonds
1 teaspoon minced fresh ginger
1 teaspoon cornstarch
2 tablespoons mirin (see page 15)
1 tablespoon soy sauce
½ pound tofu, cubed (see page 15)

Heat the oil in a heavy skillet or wok and stir in garlic and ginger. Add the leeks and stir-fry quickly over a high heat until they are bright green and tender-crisp. Whisk cornstarch together with the mirin and soy sauce and add to skillet, stirring briskly. Add tofu and stir gently until coated. Cover skillet and cook just long enough to heat through. Serve hot over steamed rice.

Sweet and Sour Leeks   SERVES 6

24 baby leeks, cut in 3-inch pieces, or 6 medium, sliced in 1-inch diamonds
2 tablespoons sesame or other oil
¼ cup water
¼ cup whole almonds (optional)
½ cup sherry vinegar or cider vinegar
2-4 tablespoons honey
2 tablespoons soy sauce
2 tablespoons cornstarch
¼ teaspoon minced fresh ginger root

Heat the oil in a wok or heavy skillet. Add the leeks and cook until their color brightens slightly. Turn, add the water, and almonds if used. Cover and cook on a low heat for five minutes.

Combine remaining ingredients. Stir briskly into the leeks and cook until the sauce thickens. Serve immediately over bowls of steaming rice.

Turkish Leeks with Rice   SERVES 6

2 tablespoons olive oil
1 medium onion, chopped
3 tablespoons whole wheat flour
1¼ cups water
1¼ cups dry white wine
6 small leeks, whole, or 3 medium, sliced lengthwise
3 cups cooked brown rice
Salt and pepper to taste

Heat the oil in a large, heavy saucepan. Add the onion and sauté until golden. Stir in the flour and cook lightly, then add the water and wine gradually to make a sauce. Stir in the cooked rice, lay the leeks on top, and sprinkle with salt and pepper. Cover pan and simmer 25 minutes or until leeks are tender.

Green Rice   SERVES 6

3 cups cooked brown rice
1 medium leek, including green top, chopped
1 cup chopped fresh parsley
1 cup grated Cheddar or Swiss cheese
1 clove garlic, minced
2 eggs, separated
1½ cups evaporated milk or half and half
¼ cup oil
Salt and pepper to taste
Juice and grated rind of one lemon
Paprika

Combine the first five ingredients and place in a buttered 2-quart baking dish. Beat the egg yolks and combine with the milk, oil, salt and pepper, and lemon. Stir into the rice mixture. Beat the egg whites until they form soft peaks, then fold gently into casserole. Sprinkle with paprika and bake at 300 degrees for 45 minutes.

Leek Bubble and Squeak   SERVES 6 TO 8

Bubble and Squeak is an English version of hash, typically made on Monday (washday) using leftover vegetables and "mash" (mashed potatoes), and served with pickles and cold cuts from Sunday's roast.

2 cups leftover cooked vegetables, such as leeks, carrots,
        cabbage, what have you
4 cups mashed potatoes
3 tablespoons oil

Mix the leftover leeks and other vegetables with mashed potatoes and fry in the oil, turning once to brown on both sides. That's it.

Potatoes and Leeks
Hashed in Cream   SERVES 6

Cooked just right, the potatoes will be like hashed browns, but creamy—light-colored on top, with a golden crust on the bottom.

2 tablespoons butter or oil
2 large leeks, chopped fine
1 medium onion, chopped fine
6 large potatoes, chopped or sliced fine
Salt and pepper to taste
1 teaspoon paprika
3 cups milk or light cream

Heat the butter or oil in a large skillet. Add the leeks and onions and sauté until tender. Stir in the potatoes, adding a little more fat if they begin to stick. Sprinkle salt, pepper, and paprika over the top, add the cream, and stir again. Cover pan and set it in a 375-degree oven for 45 minutes, or cook very slowly on top of the stove.

Leek and Potato Fritters

For each fritter:
2 tablespoons butter or oil
1 small leek, sliced into thin rings
1 medium potato
Salt and pepper to taste

Heat the oil or butter in a heavy skillet. Add the leek and sauté lightly. Grate the potato over the top, and sprinkle with salt and pepper. Fry until golden brown, turning once.

This is delicious served for breakfast with a dollop of applesauce and a dab of sour cream on top.

SEVEN

Main Dishes with Meat, Poultry, and Seafood

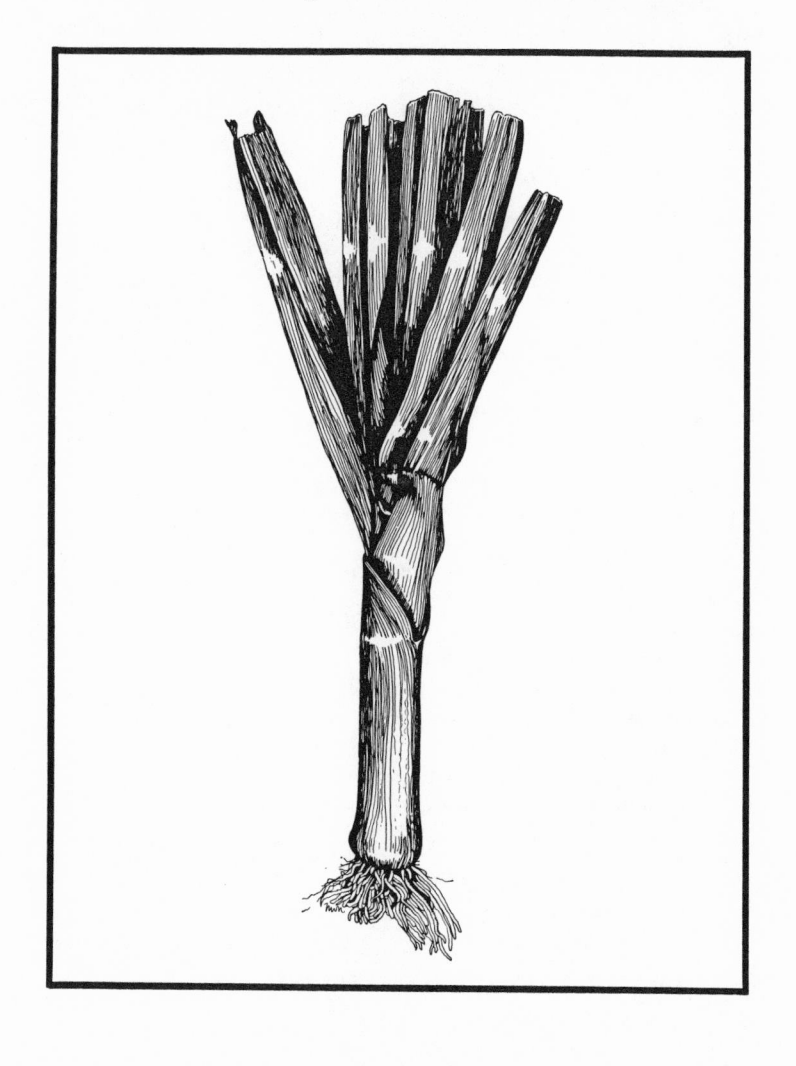

LIKE their more pungent relative, garlic, leeks enhance the flavor of any kind of meat—beef, pork, lamb or chicken—as well as fish and shellfish. Their use is traditional with some meat dishes: in Britain, for example, a lamb stew without leeks would hardly be considered lamb stew at all. Leeks also give new appeal to familiar favorites—as in Pot Roast with Leeks, or Mom's Baked Spareribs—and add interest and flavor to more exotic dishes—such as Vietnamese Stir-Fried Leeks (Tỏi Tây Xaò Thịt Bò) or Greek Pastitsia. Some recipes, like Jo's Special, are satisfying for breakfast, lunch or dinner, and simple enough to make on car camping trips. Others can be the highlight of a memorable meal. Once you have tried a few of these, don't be surprised to find yourself improving some of your favorite main dishes by making them with leeks!

Beef Bourguignon   SERVES 6

6 strips of bacon
2 pounds beef stew meat
Salt and pepper to taste
1 cup burgundy or other dry red wine
1 cup cold water or stock
2 medium onions, chopped
2 large leeks, cut in 1½-inch pieces
¾ pound fresh mushrooms, sliced
2 tablespoons oil
2 cups baby carrots
¼ cup chopped fresh parsley
3 tablespoons whole wheat flour

Fry the bacon in a Dutch oven, remove and drain. Season the beef with salt and pepper and brown it well in the bacon grease. Add the wine and water, using a little more water if necessary to cover meat. Add the onions, bring to a boil, and simmer over a very low heat for 2 to 3 hours until meat is tender.

Sauté the leeks and mushrooms in the oil. Steam the carrots separately. Add all the vegetables and the chopped parsley to the meat. Shake the flour with about 1 cup water in a jar with a tight-fitting lid and stir in gradually. Cook until the vegetables are tender, another 30 to 45 minutes. Serve over mashed or cubed potatoes, or new potatoes in season—or over noodles or rice.

Pot Roast with Leeks
SERVES 6

3 to 4 pounds fresh or frozen pot roast
1 cup coffee, tomato juice, or dry red wine
1 cup water or stock
¼ teaspoon black pepper
1 bay leaf
5 medium leeks, cut in 1-1½-inch diamonds
5 medium potatoes, whole or in chunks
5 carrots, cut in thick slices
1 medium onion, quartered

Wipe the fresh or frozen (unthawed) pot roast and place in a Dutch oven. Add the liquid, pepper, and bay leaf. Cover and cook on stove top over a very low heat, or in the oven at 300 degrees, for 2½ hours. More water or stock may be added if necessary.

Add the vegetables and cook 45 minutes to 1 hour longer, until the meat is very tender and the vegetables are done. Skim or pour off any excess fat before serving.

Vietnamese Stir-Fried Leeks
(Tỏi Tây Xaò Thịt Bò)

SERVES 4

¼ pound beef sirloin, sliced thin
1 tablespoon soy sauce
1 teaspoon cornstarch
½ teaspoon honey
1 green onion, chopped
2 tablespoons oil
½ small onion, chopped
2 medium leeks, cut in 1½-inch pieces

Marinate the beef in a mixture of soy sauce, cornstarch, honey, and green onion for about 10 minutes. Heat oil in a wok or heavy skillet over a high heat. Add the onion and sauté until golden. Add the meat and cook for 5 minutes, stirring briskly. Add the leeks and stir-fry just a few minutes—they should still be crunchy. Serve immediately over hot, steamed rice.

French Meat Balls

SERVES 4 TO 6

Small, unseasoned meatballs simmered with vegetables in beef stock.

2 large leeks, sliced in 1-inch chunks
2 medium potatoes, sliced thin
6 small carrots, sliced thin
1 large clove garlic, minced
1 pound lean ground beef
Bacon drippings
1 cup beef stock or consommé
Salt and pepper to taste

Place the leeks, potatoes, carrots, and garlic in the bottom of a baking dish. Shape the beef into small balls and sauté lightly in the bacon drippings. Lay the meatballs over the vegetables and pour the stock over all.

Sprinkle with salt and pepper, cover and bake for 30 minutes at 400 degrees. Stir gently. Taste the vegetables to be sure they are tender, and bake uncovered for 15 minutes longer.

Stovetop Meatloaf

SERVES 6

Saves using the oven on a hot summer's day, though you may want to pop the cooked loaf under the broiler for a few minutes.

2 pounds lean ground beef
1 medium leek, minced
½ cup tomato sauce
1 egg, beaten
1 cup dry bread crumbs
¼ to ½ cup water
1 large clove garlic, minced
Pinch of dry mustard
Dash of Worchestershire sauce
Salt and pepper to taste
3 strips bacon
¼ cup boiling water

Combine all ingredients except the bacon and boiling water and shape into a loaf. Place in a skillet and lay the bacon strips across top. Cover tightly and cook on stove top over a low heat for 45 minutes.

Remove bacon and set aside. Brown the loaf under broiler if desired, and transfer to a serving dish. Crumble bacon back into the skillet, adding boiling water to the pan juices. Stir well, scraping bottom of the pan. Pour this natural gravy over the meatloaf and serve.

Szekely Goulash with Leeks   SERVES 6 TO 8

1½ pounds beef
½ pound pork
½ pound veal
2 tablespoons oil
3 large leeks, sliced in 1-inch rounds
1½ quarts sauerkraut, washed and drained
1½ tablespoons paprika
1 pint sour cream

Cut the meat into bite-sized chunks and set aside. Heat the oil in a heavy skillet or Dutch oven. Sauté leeks lightly, remove from heat, and add the paprika, stirring well. Add the meat and brown. Stir in sauerkraut and cook 2 to 3 hours until meat is very tender. Stir in 1 cup sour cream just before serving, and place an additional dollop of sour cream on each serving.

Mom's Baked Spareribs

2 to 3 pounds lean spareribs
2 to 3 medium leeks, cut in 2-inch pieces
1 green pepper, seeded and diced
¼ cup soy sauce
¼ cup honey
2 tablespoons vinegar
Dash of cayenne pepper
1 medium can pineapple chunks, undrained

Brown the ribs in a heavy skillet, using a little oil to prevent sticking. Remove the ribs and pour most of the fat out of the pan, leaving ¼ cup or less. Sauté the leeks and pepper in the remaining fat until tender.

Combine the soy sauce, honey, vinegar, and cayenne in a separate saucepan and heat until honey becomes liquid, stirring occasionally. Transfer the leeks and green pepper to a shallow roasting pan, add pineapple chunks, then lay the ribs on top. Pour the sauce over all and bake at 350 degrees for 1½ to 2 hours or until the meat is tender.

Jo's Special

Variations of this recipe abound.

1 pound fresh spinach, or 1 10-ounce package frozen
2 slices bacon, chopped
4 or 5 mushrooms, sliced
2 medium leeks, in thick slices
1 pound hamburger
Salt and pepper to taste
4 to 8 eggs, well beaten
Grated Parmesan cheese

Wash and chop the spinach and cook in about ½ cup boiling water for 5 minutes. (If using frozen spinach, follow package directions.) Drain and press out liquid.

Fry the bacon in a heavy skillet, add mushrooms, and sauté lightly. Pour out most of the bacon grease. Add the leeks and sauté until barely tender, then add the hamburger, salt and pepper, and fry until the meat turns pink. Stir in the beaten eggs and spinach, and scramble gently until the eggs and meat are done. Sprinkle with grated Parmesan, and serve immediately.

Pastitsia

1 pound whole wheat macaroni or other small pasta
2 pounds lean ground beef
2 large leeks, chopped
1 large onion, chopped
Simple Tomato Sauce (below)
8 fresh tomatoes, or 4 cups canned, peeled and coarsely
       chopped
1 teaspoon cinnamon
¼ teaspoon cloves
2 teaspoons chili powder
Salt and pepper to taste
1 tablespoon butter
1 cup or more grated Parmesan cheese
Egg Sauce (below)

Cook the macaroni in boiling water until tender; drain. Fry the beef with the leeks and onion. Add 1 cup of Simple Tomato Sauce, the chopped tomatoes and seasonings, and simmer for 30 minutes.

Spoon ⅔ of the cooked macaroni into a buttered 9-by-12 baking dish. Dot with butter and sprinkle with ½ cup of the Parmesan cheese. Cover with the meat and tomato mixture. Spoon on the remaining macaroni and sprinkle with the other ½ cup of Parmesan. Pour the Egg Sauce over all and bake 40 to 60 minutes at 325 degrees. Serve with a pitcher of the remaining Tomato Sauce and pass around more Parmesan.

If you wish to make this ahead and freeze it, put it in the freezer after pouring on the Egg Sauce.

Simple Tomato Sauce

1 large can tomato juice
1 green pepper, diced
1 onion, chopped

Simmer together ½ hour or longer.

Egg Sauce

6 tablespoons butter
¾ cup wholewheat flour
1 teaspoon salt
1 quart milk
3 eggs, well beaten

Melt butter in frying pan and stir in flour and salt. Cook, stirring, until blended. Stir in milk gradually and continue stirring constantly until thick and bubbly. Add a little of this mixture to the eggs, then stir eggs into pan and cook 1 minute.

Szechuan Pork

SERVES 4 TO 6

A Chinese classic.

1 pound lean pork, cut in bite-sized pieces
½ cup water
1 teaspoon honey
¼ cup hoisin sauce*
3 tablespoons sesame or other oil
2 cloves garlic, minced
1½ teaspoons minced fresh ginger
2 medium leeks, cut in 2-inch diamonds
½ cup chopped sweet red pepper
½ cup diced firm tofu (see page 15)
¼ teaspoon cayenne pepper

Combine the water, honey, and hoisin sauce, and simmer the pork in it while you prepare the other ingredients. Heat the oil in a heavy skillet or wok and sauté the garlic and ginger for 1 minute. Add the leeks, red pepper, tofu, and cayenne. Cook 5 minutes, stirring often. Add the pork and hoisin mixture, and simmer until the leeks are tender. Serve over hot, steamed rice.

*Hoisin is a sweet, spicy sauce sometimes called the tomato catsup of the Orient. It is made from fermented soybeans with rice, garlic, sugar and spices, and is available in specialty shops.

Lamb and Leek Stew

SERVES 6

2 pounds lamb, chunked
Boiling water to cover
Salt and pepper to taste
1 bay leaf
1 teaspoon dried dill weed
5 medium leeks, in 1½-inch slices
2 large potatoes, cubed, or 10 small new potatoes
3 large carrots, sliced
3 stalks celery, cut in 1-inch slices
1 clove garlic, minced
1 cup fresh or frozen peas
2 tablespoons whole wheat flour

Pour the boiling water over the meat and bring to a boil. Skim off fat and add the seasonings. Simmer until the lamb is tender, about 1 hour.

Add the vegetables, except peas, and simmer 30 minutes. Stir in the peas, sprinkle with the flour, and simmer for another 10 minutes, stirring occasionally.

Shish Kebabs   SERVES 6

Oven-broiling is quick and easy for these, though they're best cooked over a charcoal fire.

1½-pounds shoulder, leg, or breast of lamb
Marinade (below)
Leeks, cut in 1½-inch pieces
Cherry tomatoes
Button mushrooms
Pineapple chunks
Olive oil

Cut the lamb into 1-inch cubes and let stand for at least 1 hour in the marinade. Thread the lamb chunks on skewers, alternating with the vegetables. Brush lightly with olive oil and oven-broil 10 to 15 minutes—or cook over a charcoal fire—turning frequently, until tender.

Marinade

½ cup soy sauce
¼ cup white wine or orange juice
1-2 tablespoons honey
½ teaspoon fresh ginger, minced
1 clove garlic, mashed

Armenian Chicken

SERVES 6

6 tablespoons butter
1 large onion, chopped
6 small leeks, cut in 2-inch lengths
3 medium carrots, sliced
1 small zucchini, sliced
3 large fresh tomatoes, peeled and chopped
1 large frying chicken
Salt and pepper to taste
1 tablespoon chopped parsley
1 to 2 teaspoons dried tarragon
¼ cup dry white wine
¼ pound button mushrooms, cleaned and trimmed

Sauté the onion in 2 tablespoons of the butter until transparent. Add the leeks, carrots, zucchini, and tomatoes. Cover and simmer very gently while you oven-fry the chicken as follows: Grease a large, shallow roasting pan. Sprinkle the chicken with salt and pepper. Melt the remaining butter and add the herbs, then slowly stir in the wine. Place the chicken in the pan and bake at 350 degrees for an hour, basting with the butter mixture every 15 minutes.

Half an hour before serving, add the mushrooms to the vegetables. Thin with a little wine or water if necessary. When the chicken is done, transfer the vegetables to an oven-proof serving dish or tureen, top with the chicken, and pour ¼ cup of the drippings from the chicken pan over all. Return to oven until heated through and serve.

Chicken and Leeks Oriental   SERVES 6

2½ pound frying chicken, cut up
3 tablespoons soy sauce
2 tablespoons sherry or mirin (see page 15)
¼ cup sesame or other oil
1 clove garlic, mashed
2 teaspoons minced fresh ginger
6 medium leeks, cut in 2-inch diamond slices
1 cup celery, sliced on diagonal
3 minced shallots
½ cup water
2 teaspoons cornstarch

Prepare ingredients in advance and work quickly, so the vegetables will be cooked until just tender-crisp.

Marinate the chicken pieces in the soy sauce and sherry or mirin. Heat the oil in a heavy skillet or wok, and add the garlic and ginger. Stir-fry for 1 minute, then add the chicken, leeks, celery, and shallots, in that order, stirring constantly.

Combine the water and cornstarch, and add to the remaining marinade mixture. Pour into the skillet, stirring briskly until the sauce is clear and vegetables are coated. Serve with rice.

Gourmet Chicken Livers with Leeks   SERVES 4 TO 6

4 medium leeks, sliced thin
3 tablespoons butter or oil
2½ tablespoons paprika
2 pounds chicken livers
3 tablespoons marsala
1½ cups sour cream
Salt and pepper to taste

Sauté the leeks in the butter or oil until soft and beginning to brown. Add the paprika and mix well. Add the livers and sauté until done, stirring often but gently to avoid breaking livers. Remove from heat and stir in the marsala. Cook 5 minutes, mix in the sour cream, and season with salt and pepper. Simmer for another 5 minutes. Serve over hot, steamed rice and top with a dollop of applesauce.

Fish and Leeks Baked in Wine   SERVES 4

2 medium leeks, finely sliced
2 tablespoons grated onion
3 tablespoons butter
Salt and pepper to taste
2 cups dry white wine
2 pounds sole, halibut, or other white fish fillets
2 cups cooked shrimp (optional)
¼ to ½ cup buttered bread crumbs

Sauté the leeks and onion in butter, sprinkle with salt and pepper, and add the wine. Simmer 5 minutes. Lay the fish fillets in the bottom of a baking dish and cover with the shrimp. Pour the vegetables and wine over all. Sprinkle with the bread crumbs and bake 20 to 30 minutes in a 350-degree oven.

Barcelona Fish   SERVES 4 TO 6

¼ cup olive oil
2 tomatoes, sliced very thin
1 green pepper, coarsely chopped
2 large leeks, sliced very thin
2 pounds halibut, cod, or sea bass
24 Greek olives
2 cloves garlic, minced
½ teaspoon saffron
¼ cup dry white wine
2 large potatoes, sliced paper thin
Salt and pepper to taste
Paprika

Rub a teaspoon of the olive oil around the sides and bottom of a large casserole dish. Lay the tomatoes on the bottom of dish, then the pepper, then leeks. Cut the fish in 1-inch strips and place on top of the leeks, then sprinkle the olives and garlic over the fish. Add the saffron to the wine and pour over all.

Arrange the potatoes over the dish, drizzle with remaining olive oil, season with salt and pepper, and sprinkle with paprika. Bake uncovered at 300 degrees until the potatoes are tender and golden, 45 to 60 minutes.

Priscilla's Steamed Clams SERVES 4

4 pounds fresh butter clams, scrubbed
1½ to 2 cups white wine
1 medium leek, minced
½ cup minced fresh parsley

Place the clams in a large stockpot and add the wine to a depth of about ½ inch on the bottom of the pot. Sprinkle the minced leeks over the clams, cover the pot tightly, and steam for 5 to 10 minutes until the clams open.

Just before serving, sprinkle the parsley over the cooked clams. The cooking stock makes a delicious clam broth which can be enjoyed plain or used as a stock in cooking.

Oysters Gilma SERVES 4

¼ cup butter
1 small leek, finely chopped
2 teaspoons dried tarragon
1 tablespoon minced fresh parsley
1 clove garlic, minced
2 cups shelled fresh oysters
Bread crumbs

Heat the butter in a small skillet, add the leek, herbs, and garlic, and sauté gently. Lay the oysters in an attractive baking dish. Pour the butter mixture over the oysters, top with bread crumbs, and bake at 350 degrees for 5 to 10 minutes.

Alternatively, add the oysters to the butter and leek in a skillet, and fry gently 5 to 10 minutes until done. Any extra butter mixture is delicious over a baked potato.

Seafood Crêpes Anne Marie

Expensive, but when you want to pull out all the stops, this can hardly be beat.

Seafood Sauce

3 medium leeks
¼ to ½ pound fresh mushrooms
2 tablespoons butter
1½ cups Cream Sauce (see page 25)
1 cup grated Swiss or Gruyère cheese
12 large shrimp (or 1 can)
½ pound crab (or 1 can)
¼ to ½ pound scallops
1 to 2 tablespoons dry sherry (optional)

Slice the leeks in ½-inch pieces, reserving ¼ cup minced green tops for garnish. Slice the mushrooms, and sauté with the leeks in the butter.

In a separate saucepan, heat the Cream Sauce until bubbly. Stir the vegetables into sauce, add cheese, and mix well. Gradually stir in the seafood, and sherry if used. Simmer until heated through.

Put a bit of the seafood mixture on each crêpe (see below), roll up and place in a buttered baking dish. Pour remaining sauce over top and bake at 350 degrees for 15 minutes until piping hot. The seafood sauce is also superb over plain steamed brown rice, buttered noodles, or toast.

Crêpes

2 eggs
1 cup milk
¾ cup wholewheat flour
1 tablespoon melted butter or oil

Place all ingredients in a blender or mixing bowl and whirl until smooth. Cover and let stand 1 hour or longer, preferably overnight.

Heat a small pan and oil it lightly. Pour in just enough crêpe batter to cover the pan with a thin layer, tilting pan to spread evenly. Cook until just set, turn, and cook until second side is browned. Remove onto a flat surface covered with a smooth cloth, fill, and roll up. This makes enough batter for about 18 crêpes.

EIGHT

Meatless Main Dishes

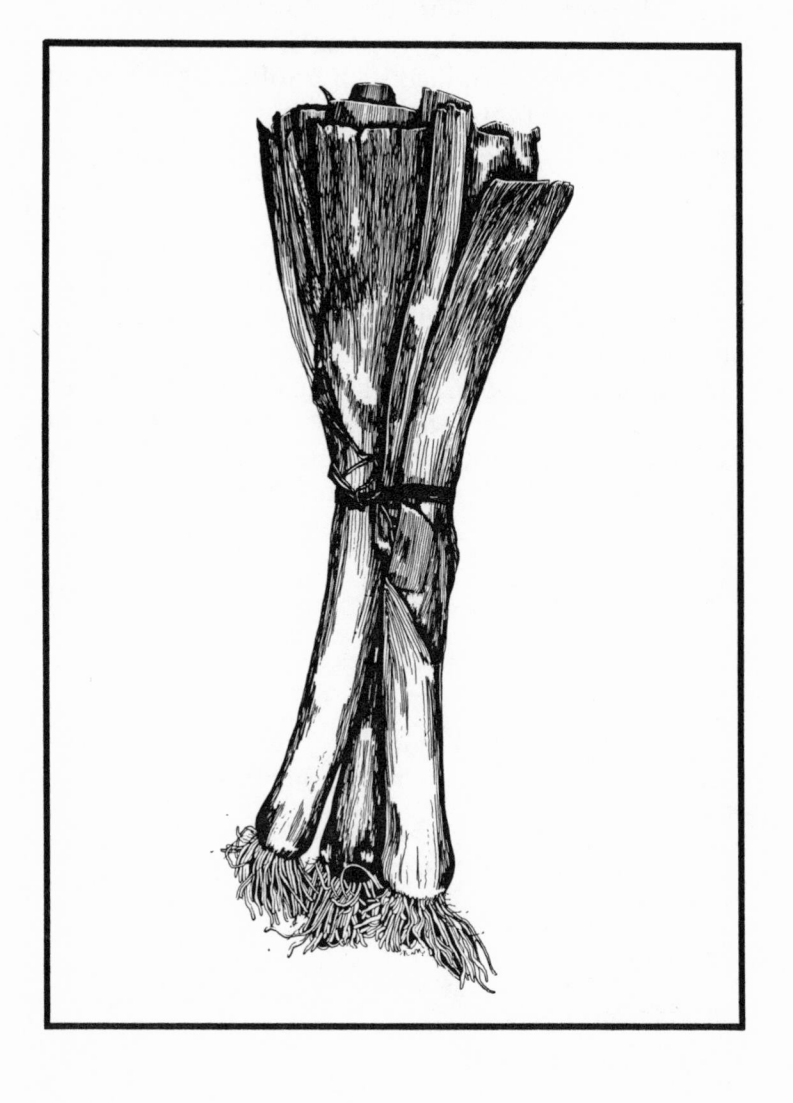

CREATIVE cooks can discover uses for leeks in a variety of vegetarian entrées so tasty and interesting that meat will never be missed. A totally vegetarian diet takes careful planning, of course, but anyone can enjoy meatless dishes occasionally—whether for economy, variety, or to accommodate others' preferences. Leeks go well with milk, eggs, cheese, grains and nuts, and beans or legumes (including soybean products such as tofu). When used in judicious combinations, these foods can provide adequate dietary protein.

Though meat may be added to many of these recipes, without it the subtle flavor of leeks plays a more pronounced yet never overpowering role. The term "casserole" hardly does justice to some of the entrées offered here, such as Zucchini-Leek Moussaka, spiced with cinnamon and baked with a cottage cheese custard sauce. The happy combination of leeks and eggs is the basis for many tasty main dishes which can be served any time of day—Tender Leek Frittata for dinner, Leek Foo Yung for lunch, or Leek and Eggs Chasseur for breakfast.

Pasta Rustica
SERVES 6 TO 8

2 medium leeks, including green tops
2 medium carrots
1 large onion
1 cup fresh parsley, packed down
3 tablespoons fresh basil, or 1 tablespoon dried
¼ cup olive oil
3 large tomatoes, or 2 cups canned, peeled and chopped
½ head small cabbage, chopped
3 stalks celery, chopped
2 medium zucchinis, chopped
1 cup stock
2 cups cooked white beans
Salt and pepper to taste

2 cups whole wheat small pasta
3 tablespoons butter
½ cup grated Parmesan cheese

Mince the leeks, carrots, onion, parsley, and basil together on a board. Heat the olive oil in a large, heavy saucepan and cook the vegetable mixture in it for about 7 minutes or until tender, stirring often. Add remaining vegetables and stock to the saucepan, cover, and simmer about 10 minutes. Stir in the cooked beans, salt and pepper and heat through.

Cook the pasta in boiling water until tender, drain, and toss together with the butter and cheese. Combine with the vegetables and serve hot.

Lentil and Leek Supper Dish   SERVES 6

2 tablespoons oil or butter
2 large carrots, sliced
2 medium leeks, cut in thick slices
2 cups dried lentils, preferably golden variety
6 cups tomato juice
½ teaspoon cinnamon
¼ teaspoon nutmeg
1 large clove garlic, minced
½ teaspoon celery seed
1 bay leaf
Salt and pepper to taste
Grated Parmesan cheese

Heat the oil or butter in a large stockpot and sauté the carrots until nearly tender. Add the leeks and continue to cook for about 5 minutes, stirring occasionally. Add remaining ingredients, except for the cheese, and simmer until tender, about 45 minutes. Ladle into bowls, sprinkle with Parmesan cheese, and serve with French bread.

Zucchini-Leek Moussaka

SERVES 6

An extremely variable dish, and much easier than it looks.

3 tablespoons oil or butter
5 medium potatoes, sliced
1 large onion, minced
2 large leeks, in 1½-inch chunks
2 medium zucchini, sliced lengthwise or in rounds
3 fresh tomatoes, peeled and chopped
¼ cup chopped fresh parsley
½ teaspoon cinnamon
2 cups milk (part cream if desired)
¼ cup whole wheat flour
3 eggs, well beaten
1 cup ricotta or cottage cheese
¼ teaspoon nutmeg
Salt and pepper to taste

Heat the oil or butter in a large, heavy skillet or Dutch oven. Add the potatoes, onion, and leeks, and sauté until nearly soft. Add the zucchini and cook until almost tender. Combine the tomatoes with the parsley and cinnamon and add to the vegetable mixture. Simmer 5 minutes, then transfer to a casserole and bake 20 minutes at 350 degrees.

Shake the milk in a jar with flour, beat into the eggs, and add the cheese and seasonings. Pour the mixture over the moussaka and bake for another 10 minutes, or until top is browned and bubbly.

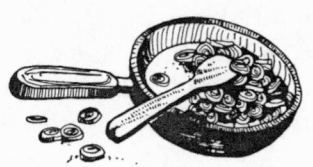

Leek and Mushroom Stew

SERVES 6

2½ cups cold water
5 large carrots, sliced
5 medium potatoes, diced
2 large leeks, sliced in 1-inch diamonds
½ pound mushrooms, sliced
2 teaspoons finely minced fresh ginger
3 tablespoons soy sauce
2 tablespoons whole wheat flour

Bring 2 cups of the water to a boil in a large, heavy saucepan. Add the vegetables in the order given, waiting a few minutes between each addition (you can chop as you go along). Reduce heat to a simmer.

Place the ginger and soy sauce in a small jar with a tight-fitting lid, add the remaining ½ cup of cold water and then the flour. Shake vigorously till smooth, then pour into the stew and stir well. Simmer for about 20 minutes, stirring occasionally.

Pizza Leeky with Spaghetti Crust

SERVES 6

A delicious way to use leftover spaghetti. Also good with a regular whole wheat crust, of course.

Spaghetti Crust

1 egg
¼ cup milk
½ cup grated mozzarella cheese
1 clove garlic, minced
½ pound whole wheat spaghetti, cooked and drained

Combine all the ingredients and spread into a greased pizza or jelly roll pan, pushing up along the sides. Bake at 350 degrees for 15 minutes, then spread with topping.

Topping

3 tablespoons olive oil
4 medium leeks, in ¼-inch slices
1 clove garlic, minced
1 cup tomato paste
½ teaspoon dried oregano
Salt and pepper to taste
½ to 1 cup water
½ cup sliced black olives
½ cup sliced mushrooms
¼ to ½ pound mozzarella cheese, grated

Sauté the leeks and garlic in 2 tablespoons of the oil until tender. Remove half of the leeks and reserve. Stir in the tomato paste, seasonings, and water, and simmer about 15 minutes.

Assemble pizza by spreading the tomato-leek sauce on the crust and arranging the olives, mushrooms and sautéed leeks on top. Brush with remaining olive oil, top with mozzarella cheese, sprinkle on a little more oregano, and bake 25 minutes at 425 degrees.

Spaghetti with Fresh Peas and Leeks
SERVES 4 TO 6

2 large leeks
1 medium onion
1 clove garlic
1 stalk celery
1 bunch parsley
3 tablespoons olive oil
3 tablespoons butter
1½ pounds fresh peas
½ cup stock or tomato juice
1 large tomato, peeled and chopped
2 tablespoons chopped fresh basil
Salt and pepper to taste
2 to 3 quarts boiling water
½ pound spaghetti
Grated Parmesan cheese

Chop the leeks, onion, garlic, celery, and parsley together on a board. Heat the oil and butter in a large frying pan or Dutch oven and add the chopped ingredients. Cook gently for about 10 minutes. Add the peas and stock and simmer, covered, until the peas are tender. Towards the end of cooking, add the chopped tomato and seasonings.

Cook the spaghetti in boiling water until tender, and drain well. Toss the vegetables with the hot spaghetti and serve with lots of grated Parmesan cheese.

Leekaroni and Cheese   SERVES 6

2 cups whole wheat macaroni (8 ounces dry)
2 to 3 quarts boiling water
2 medium leeks, thinly sliced
1 cup sliced mushrooms
2 tablespoons butter or oil
2 cups Cream Sauce (see page 25)
2 cups cream-style cottage cheese
1 to 2 teaspoons dry mustard
Salt and pepper to taste
2 cups grated Cheddar cheese
¼ cup finely chopped fresh parsley

Stir the macaroni into the boiling water and cook until tender, about 15 minutes. Drain the noodles well and place half of it in an oiled 2-quart baking dish.

Sauté the vegetables in butter until almost tender. Stir in the Cream Sauce, cottage cheese, seasonings, 1½ cups of the Cheddar cheese, and the parsley. Pour half of this sauce over the noodles, cover with the remaining macaroni and top with the rest of the sauce. Bake 20 minutes at 350 degrees. Sprinkle remaining Cheddar cheese over the top and return to oven until the cheese is melted, about 5 minutes.

Toasted Cheese and Leek Sandwiches

These sandwiches, with a hearty soup and a salad, make one of our favorite winter meals.

For each sandwich:

2 slices whole wheat bread
Butter or margarine
German mustard
1 slice sharp Cheddar cheese
2 to 3 tablespoons cooked, drained (or leftover) leeks

Butter the outsides of the bread and spread mustard on the insides. Place the cheese on one slice of bread, top with the leeks and the second slice of bread. Fry over a medium-low heat until the bread is toasted, flip and fry again until the cheese melts and the sandwich is golden brown.

Leek and Mushroom Business
SERVES 6 TO 8

In one form or another, this has been a part of our family holiday dinners for years.

¾ pound mushrooms, cleaned
3 medium leeks, cut in 1½-inch chunks
4 tablespoons butter
8 slices whole wheat bread
½ cup finely chopped onion
½ cup finely chopped celery
½ cup finely chopped green pepper
½ cup mayonnaise
Salt and pepper to taste
2 eggs, slightly beaten
1½ cups milk
2 cups thick Cream Sauce (see page 25)
1 cup grated Swiss or Cheddar cheese

Sauté the mushrooms with the leeks in 2 tablespoons of the butter. Spread part of the remaining butter on 3 slices of the bread and cut into 1-inch squares. Line a large baking dish with the bread squares. Mix the leeks and mushrooms with the next five ingredients and spread over the bread. Butter and cut 3 more slices of bread and layer over the vegetables. Mix the beaten eggs with milk and pour over all.

Refrigerate the casserole at least 1 hour, perferably overnight. Then butter the last 2 slices of bread, cut in ½-inch squares, and place on top. Spoon the Cream Sauce over all and bake at 325 degrees for 50 to 60 minutes. Before serving, sprinkle with the grated cheese and return to the oven until the cheese is melted.

Leek Foo Yung

SERVES 4

4 eggs
1 medium leek sliced very thin, or green tops of 2
1 cup fresh bean sprouts
½ cup sliced mushrooms
½ cup Jerusalem artichokes, sliced in matchsticks
1 tablespoon peanut or other oil
Soy sauce

Beat the eggs well and stir in the leeks, sprouts, mushrooms and Jerusalem artichokes. Heat the oil in a heavy skillet and fry egg mixture in small batches, turning once to brown both sides. Add more oil for cooking if necessary. Serve with soy sauce. Any leftovers are great packed in a lunch.

Leek Fried Rice

SERVES 6

2 tablespoons oil
4 cups cooked brown rice (leftovers are fine)
1 medium leek, or green tops of 2, thinly sliced
½ teaspoon chopped fresh ginger
1 cup bean sprouts
½ pound tofu, cubed (see page 15)
3 eggs, well beaten
2 tablespoons soy sauce

Heat the oil in a large, heavy skillet. Add the cooked rice and fry lightly, separating the grains with a fork. Add the leek and ginger, cook briefly, then stir in the bean sprouts and tofu. Sauté lightly, then push the rice mixture to the side of the skillet and add a little more oil to the center. Pour in the eggs and scramble them, then mix the rice with the eggs. Sprinkle with the soy sauce and serve hot.

Tender Leek Frittata

SERVES 6

Vary this dish by using peppers, artichoke hearts, olives, green beans, tomatoes, or other fresh vegetables.

1 medium leek, julienned
½ cup sliced mushrooms
1 medium zucchini, cut in matchsticks
½ cup chopped fresh spinach
1 large clove garlic, minced
1 tablespoon lemon juice
2 tablespoons butter
¼ to ½ cup white wine or water
6 eggs, lightly beaten
Salt and pepper to taste
3 tablespoons minced chervil or parsley
½ cup grated Parmesan, Cheddar, mozzarella or other cheese

Poach the vegetables gently in the lemon juice, butter, and wine until tender. Begin with ¼ cup of liquid and add more if necessary; the pan juices should be absorbed when the leeks are tender.

Combine the eggs and seasonings and pour into the pan. Cook slowly until set, lifting outer edges so the uncooked part runs beneath. Top with grated cheese and set under broiler until melted. Serve in wedges, hot or cold.

Leek and Eggs Chasseur   SERVES 4

Deluxe for breakfast, fine for a luncheon or light supper, too.

1 medium leek, finely chopped
2 shallots, finely chopped
½ cup sliced mushrooms
2 tablespoons minced fresh parsley
2 tablespoons butter
Salt and pepper to taste
1 cup light cream
2 tablespoons fine whole wheat flour
2 tablespoons sherry
4 eggs, hardboiled and sliced
Toast for four servings
½ cup grated Parmesan cheese (optional)

In a medium frying pan, cook the leek, shallots, mushrooms, and parsley in butter for about 10 minutes. Combine the seasonings with the cream, sherry and flour in a pint jar and shake to blend, then add to the pan and heat slowly until thickened, stirring often. Lay the sliced hardboiled eggs on top and heat through. Serve over toast, with Parmesan cheese sprinkled on top if desired.

Leek and Mushroom Bake

SERVES 4

¼ cup butter or oil
2 medium leeks, thinly sliced
1 pound mushrooms, sliced
Salt and pepper to taste
2 tablespoons whole wheat flour
1 cup grated Swiss cheese
2 egg yolks
2 cups light cream
½ cup buttered whole wheat bread crumbs

Melt the butter in a skillet, add the leeks, and cook slowly 10 to 15 minutes. Add the mushrooms and cook until wilted. Sprinkle with salt and pepper. Stir in the flour and cheese, then place in a buttered 2-quart baking dish. Beat the egg yolks with cream and pour over the mushroom mixture. Top with the bread crumbs and bake 30 minutes at 350 degrees, or until set.

Piperade

SERVES 6

A hearty open omelette, Basque style.

¼ cup olive oil
3 large potatoes, cooked and sliced
2 medium leeks, thinly sliced
1 red or green sweet pepper, sliced
4 medium tomatoes, peeled and chopped
6 to 8 eggs, well beaten
½ teaspoon dried thyme or marjoram
Salt and pepper to taste

Heat the oil in large skillet and sauté the potatoes and leeks until they begin to brown lightly. Add the sweet pepper and tomatoes and continue to cook until tender. Combine the remaining ingredients and pour over the vegetables. Scramble gently over low heat until the eggs are set.

Balkan Vegetable Medley   SERVES 6 TO 8

1 large onion, sliced
2 large carrots, thinly sliced
2 medium potatoes, sliced
2 large leeks, sliced in 1-inch rounds or diamonds
½ cup lima or broad beans, fresh or frozen
1 cup corn, fresh or frozen
1 cup summer or winter squash, diced
4 large tomatoes, or 2 cups canned, peeled and coarsely
        chopped
¼ cup chopped fresh parsley
2 cloves garlic, minced
¼ cup chopped mixed fresh herbs
Salt and pepper to taste
1 cup vegetable stock
½ cup olive oil
Sesame-Lemon Sauce (see page 27)

Combine all the vegetables and place in a large baking
pan. Sprinkle with the herbs and seasonings. In a small
saucepan, heat the stock and the oil to boiling, then pour
over the vegetables. Stir well, cover pan, and bake at 350
degrees for 1 hour, or until the vegetables are cooked and
the liquid is absorbed. Add more hot stock if necessary, or
uncover pan if there is too much liquid.

Prepare Sesame-Lemon Sauce and pour over the vegetables. Bake another 10 minutes, and serve piping hot.

NINE

Soufflés, Pies, and Quiches

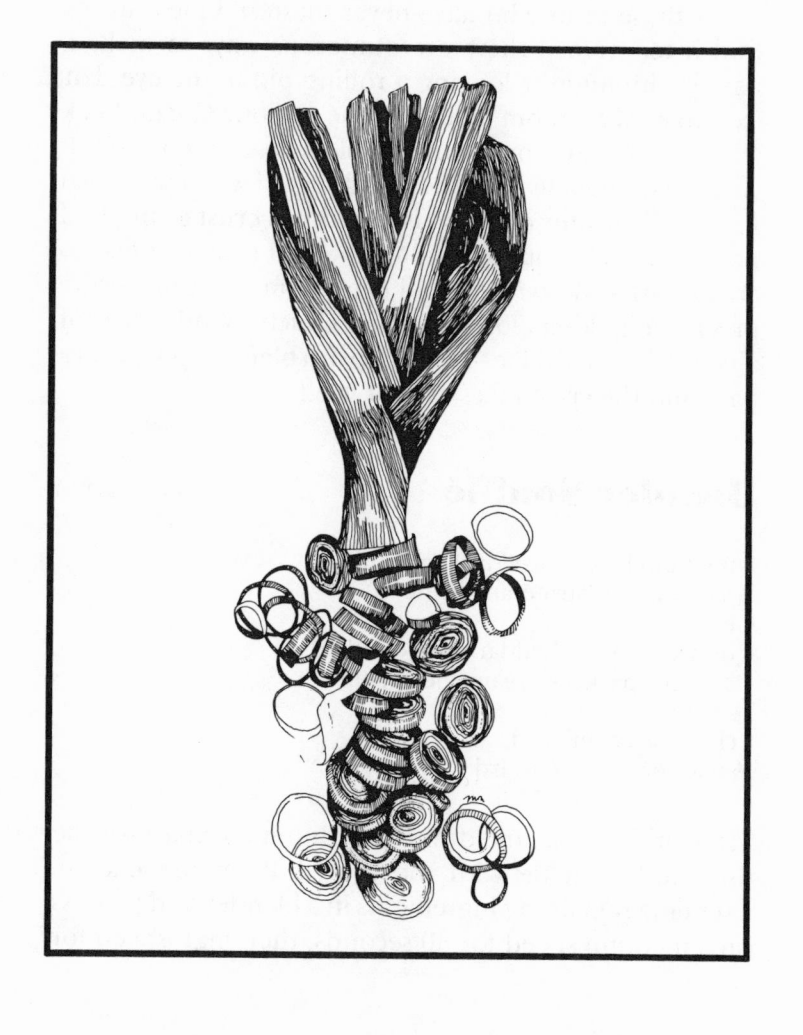

THERE are so many savory ways to enjoy leeks in a crust—with vegetables, with eggs, in a creamy or cheesy sauce, with or without meat. A favorite with our family is the Huey Special Leek Quiche, which can be made with ham, bacon, or water chestnuts. Blender Soufflé is a surprising recipe—try it once and you'll find it hard to go back to the standard method of making a soufflé.

For those of us who have never mastered pie crust or find it too greasy, there are numerous ways to make a pastry without ever looking a rolling pin in the eye. For example, Mushroom Mock Quiche or Sour Cream Leek and Sage Pie are made with whole wheat biscuit dough from a homemade mix. Shepherd's Pie, a wonderful dish for a chilly winter evening, is baked in a crust of mashed potatoes. Leek Gougère has a rich, light pastry similar to cream puffs. Brown rice and eggs form the crust of the green and golden Florentine Rice Quiche. And easiest of all is Leek Custard Pie—mix it up in a blender, pour it in a pan, and the crust takes care of itself.

Blender Soufflé   SERVES 6

2 medium leeks, sliced in 1-inch rounds
¼ cup grated Parmesan cheese
4 eggs
4 ounces sharp Cheddar cheese, cubed
1 3-ounce package cream cheese, cubed
⅓ cup milk
1 clove garlic, minced
½ teaspoon dry mustard

Steam the leeks and drain well. Butter a 1-quart soufflé dish and sprinkle with the grated Parmesan cheese. Combine remaining ingredients in a blender and process on a medium speed for 30 seconds, then high speed for

10 to 15 seconds. Place the leeks in the bottom of the soufflé dish and pour the egg mixture over them. Stir very gently and bake at 350 degrees for 25 to 30 minutes, until puffy and browned.

Mock Cheese Soufflé SERVES 6

Not really a soufflé at all—but so light and puffy it seems like one.

2 large leeks, coarsely chopped or sliced in 1-inch rounds
3 tablespoons oil or butter
6 to 8 slices whole wheat bread, torn into 2-inch pieces
3 cups grated Swiss or Cheddar cheese
4 eggs, well beaten
4 cups milk (or 2 cups milk and 2 cups dry white wine)
Salt and pepper to taste
1 teaspoon dried savory, dill, parsley, or tarragon
1 teaspoon soy sauce

Sauté the leeks in oil or butter. Meanwhile, cover the bottom of a large, buttered soufflé or baking dish with ⅓ of the bread pieces. Place ⅓ of the sautéed leeks over the bread and continue layering, ending with leeks.* Combine remaining ingredients and pour over the bread and leeks.

Cover the dish and let stand 1 hour or longer, preferably overnight. Bake in a pan of water at 300 degrees for 1 hour, and serve warm.

*1 cup of diced ham or crabmeat may be added as a layer if desired.

Leek Gougère

Pastry

1 cup water
½ cup butter or oil
Salt and pepper to taste
1 cup whole wheat flour
4 eggs
1 cup grated Swiss or Gruyère cheese (optional)

Combine the water and butter or oil in a saucepan. Bring to a boil and add the flour all at once. Cook and stir vigorously until the mixture forms a ball that doesn't separate. Remove from heat and cool 5 minutes.

Add eggs to the mixture one at a time, beating very thoroughly after each addition. Stir in the cheese if used. Spread in a buttered baking dish, pressing evenly across the bottom and sides. Bake for 20 minutes at 400 degrees. Pour the filling (below) over the pastry and bake 15 to 20 minutes longer.

Filling

1 tablespoon butter or oil
2 medium leeks, sliced in 1-inch rounds
½ cup diced green pepper
2 tablespoons chopped fresh parsley
1 clove garlic, mashed
½ cup dry red wine
1 tablespoon cornstarch
2 cups tomato purée
1 tablespoon Worcestershire sauce
1 teaspoon honey

Melt the butter in a saucepan. Add and sauté the garlic, leeks, pepper, and parsley. Dissolve the cornstarch in the wine, combine with the remaining ingredients, and stir into the pan. Continue stirring until thickened, then pour over the pastry.

Flan de Poireaux

SERVES 6

Cottage Cheese Pastry

½ cup cottage cheese
½ cup butter, softened
1 cup whole wheat pastry flour
Salt to taste

Mix all the ingredients together to make a smooth dough. Quickly and lightly press into a 9-inch pie plate, pressing up well on sides. Prick bottom and chill. Preheat oven to 425 degrees and bake shell for 10 minutes. Cool.

Filling

4 medium leeks, sliced thin
1 cup chopped crabmeat
3 whole eggs, well beaten
1 cup cream or milk
1 teaspoon curry powder
Salt to taste
Butter
½ cup grated Gruyère or Swiss cheese

Steam the leeks and drain well. Place in the prebaked pastry shell and arrange the crabmeat on top. Combine the eggs, cream, curry powder, and salt. Pour the mixture over the leeks and crab. Dab with butter and bake at 375 degrees for 25 minutes. Sprinkle with the grated cheese and bake for 5 to 10 minutes longer.

Leek and Tomato Pie

SERVES 6

Cottage Cheese Pastry for single-crust pie (see page 93)
2 teaspoons Dijon mustard
1 large or 2 medium leeks, sliced in 1-inch rounds
3 large ripe tomatoes, peeled and sliced
½ pound tofu (see page 15), well drained and mashed, or 1 cup
    ricotta cheese
¼ cup grated Parmesan cheese
Salt and pepper to taste
1 teaspoon chopped fresh rosemary, or ½ teaspoon dried
¼ cup chopped fresh parsley

Prepare the pastry according to directions for Flan de Poireaux (page 93). Brush bottom of the prebaked pie shell with mustard. Steam the leeks until just tender, and place in the pie shell. Spread the tofu or ricotta cheese over the leeks, then arrange the tomato slices on top. Sprinkle with the Parmesan cheese and seasonings. Bake at 350 degrees for 25 minutes and serve hot.

Torta Pasqualina

SERVES 6

An Italian Easter pie, with two crusts and a creamy filling.

Cream Cheese Pastry

8 ounces cream cheese, softened
1 cup butter, softened
1 egg yolk
2 cups whole wheat pastry flour

Combine the cream cheese and butter in a mixing bowl. Add the egg yolk and mix thoroughly. Work in the flour by hand to form a smooth dough. Chill.

Roll the dough out to form two crusts, and line a 9-inch pie dish with one. Pour the filling in, cover with the top crust, and flute the edges. Make 3 parallel slashes through the top crust and bake at 375 degrees for 45 minutes.

If you prefer, omit the top crust and, instead, sprinkle the pie with 1 cup grated cheese before baking.

Filling

2 large leeks, coarsely chopped
1 cup ricotta or cottage cheese
3 whole eggs, beaten
2 cups milk

Steam and drain the leeks. Combine the remaining ingredients, stir in the leeks, and pour into the prepared pastry shell.

Creamy Leek and Cauliflower Pie
SERVES 6

The delicate flavors of leeks and cauliflower are complemented here by a creamy cheese filling. Having some homemade biscuit mix and frozen or leftover cream sauce on hand makes preparation time a matter of minutes.

Whole Wheat Biscuit Mix

9 cups fine whole wheat flour
1½ cups instant dry milk
1 tablespoon salt (optional)
½ cup wheat germ
¼ cup baking powder
1½ cups magarine

Combine the dry ingredients. Cut in the margarine with two knives or a pastry blender until consistency resembles coarse meal. (Placed in an airtight container and stored in a cool place, the mix will keep 10 to 12 weeks.) For the pie crust, measure 3 cups of the mix into a bowl, make a well in the center, and add ⅔ cup milk all at once. Stir quickly with a fork until the dough forms a ball, adding a little more milk if necessary. Turn out on a lightly floured surface and knead gently. Press into a baking dish, pushing up to edges and crimping.

Filling

4 medium leeks, cut into julienne strips
1 pound fresh cauliflower, broken into pieces
1 3-ounce package cream cheese, softened
1 cup Cream Sauce (see page 15)
Salt and pepper to taste
1 cup grated sharp Cheddar cheese

Steam the leeks and cauliflower separately until tender. Drain and place in the prepared pie crust. Stir the cream cheese into the Cream Sauce, pour over the vegetables, and season with salt and pepper. Mix lightly. Bake for 25 minutes at 375 degrees, then sprinkle the grated cheese on top and return to oven for 10 minutes longer, until crust is done and pie is golden brown.

Leek Custard Pie   SERVES 6

1 large leek, or green tops of 2, coarsely chopped
4 eggs
3 cups milk (part cream if desired)
½ cup whole wheat flour
2 tablespoons butter, cut up
Seasonings to taste: nutmeg, lemon peel, pepper, paprika,
       herbs, salt

Place all the ingredients in a blender and purée for about 2 minutes, until the leeks are chopped fine. Pour immediately into a buttered 9-inch baking dish, before the flour particles settle. Bake at 300 degrees for 45 minutes or until set. Allow to stand 10 minutes before serving—or refrigerate overnight and serve cold in thin wedges as hors d'oeuvres.

Sour Cream Leek and Sage Pie

SERVES 6

Whole Wheat Biscuit Crust (see pages 95-96)
3 large leeks, cut in 1½-inch rounds or diamonds
½ to ¾ teaspoon sage, rubbed between fingers
Salt and pepper to taste
1½ cups sour cream

Prepare the biscuit crust according to directions for Creamy Leek and Cauliflower Pie (pages 95-96). Steam the leeks until tender, and place in the pie shell. Sprinkle with the sage, salt and pepper, and spread the sour cream over top. Bake at 350 degrees until the crust is golden brown, about 30 minutes.

Garden Vegetable Pie

SERVES 6

1 large head broccoli, cut in 1-inch pieces
1 large leek, sliced in thick rounds
½ cup chopped green pepper
1 cup shredded sharp Cheddar cheese
1½ cups milk
¾ cup Whole Wheat Biscuit Mix (see page 95)
3 eggs
Salt and pepper to taste

Steam the broccoli and leek until tender, about 7 minutes. Mix with the green pepper and cheese in a lightly greased 10-inch pie plate. Combine remaining ingredients, using a blender or hand beater, and pour over the vegetables. Bake at 400 degrees until golden brown and a knife comes out clean, about 35 to 40 minutes. Allow to stand 5 minutes before cutting and serving.

Shepherd's Pie   SERVES 6

6 large potatoes, peeled and quartered
½ cup milk
3 tablespoons butter
3 medium leeks, cut in thick slices
2 large carrots, sliced
3 stalks celery, chopped
1 cup mushrooms, washed and trimmed
2 tablespoons butter
1 cup fresh or frozen peas
2 cups Cream Sauce (see page 15)

Cook the potatoes and mash them, adding the milk and butter. Line a 2-quart baking dish with ⅔ of the potatoes and bake 10 minutes at 400 degrees. Cool.

Steam the leeks, carrots, and celery until tender. In a separate skillet, sauté the mushrooms with the butter. If using frozen peas, allow to thaw, then separate with a fork. Spread all of the vegetables over the bottom of the potato crust and cover with the Cream Sauce. Cover with a thin layer of the remaining mashed potatoes and bake 20 minutes at 400 degrees until golden brown. Serve piping hot.

Turkey Leeky Pot Pie   SERVES 6

A tasty solution to the leftover Thanksgiving turkey dilemma.

5 tablespoons butter or oil
5 tablespoons whole wheat flour
2½ cups turkey broth
Salt and pepper to taste
2 cups cooked, chopped turkey
2 medium leeks, sliced in 1-inch rounds
½ cup peas (fresh or leftover)
1 carrot, sliced
Pastry for single-crust pie
¼ cup heavy cream

Heat the butter or oil in a deep, heavy pan. Stir in the flour and brown lightly. Add the broth gradually, stirring constantly until smooth. Season to taste, then add the turkey, leeks, peas, and carrots. Combine thoroughly.

Place the pie crust over the mixture, cutting a 2-inch hole in the center. Bake 35 minutes in a 425-degree oven, until the crust is golden brown. Remove from oven.

Heat the cream, pour through the hole in the crust, and allow the pie to stand 10 minutes before serving.

Huey Special Leek Quiche   SERVES 6

Named after its creators, out long-time friends and neighbors, the Hueys. This can be frozen, thawed, and reheated with excellent results.

Pastry for single-crust pie
2 tablespoons oil
3 medium leeks, sliced in 1-inch rounds
½ cup chopped celery
1 cup sliced water chestnuts or 8 slices bacon, fried and
       crumbled, or 1 cup chopped ham
3 eggs, beaten
1 cup whole milk or light cream
½ teaspoon Worcestershire sauce
1 to 2 cups grated Swiss cheese

Place the pastry in a deep 10-inch pie pan. Cover with brown paper and a smaller pan to prevent bubbling. Prebake at 400 degrees for 10 minutes.

Sauté the leeks and celery in the oil. Line the prebaked crust with ham, bacon, or water chestnuts—or a combination of them—and place the leeks and celery on top. Mix the beaten eggs with the milk or cream and the Worcestershire sauce, then pour over the leeks. Top with the Swiss cheese and bake for 40 minutes at 350 degrees. Let stand for 10 minutes, then serve.

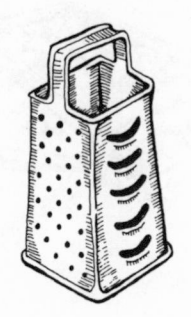

Mushroom Mock Quiche
SERVES 6

3 cups mushrooms, sliced or left whole
1 large leek, or green tops of 2, coarsely chopped
1 clove garlic, minced
2 tablespoons butter
2 cups milk
1 cup grated Swiss or Gruyère cheese
⅔ cup Whole Wheat Biscuit Mix (see page 95)
4 eggs
1 teaspoon Dijon mustard
2 teaspoons minced fresh parsley
1 teaspoon dried thyme, crumbled
Salt and pepper to taste

Sauté the mushrooms, leeks, and garlic in butter. Spoon into a 10-inch pie plate. Combine remaining ingredients and mix until smooth. Pour the mixture over the vegetables and bake at 350 degrees for 50 to 60 minutes, or until a knife comes out clean. Allow to stand for 10 minutes before cutting into wedges.

Florentine Rice Quiche
SERVES 6

2 cups cooked rice
4 eggs
1 clove garlic, minced
1 pound fresh spinach, chopped
2 medium leeks, chopped
2 tablespoons butter or oil
1 cup cottage cheese
¼ cup grated Parmesan cheese
⅓ cup heavy cream or evaporated milk
Pinch of cayenne pepper
¼ teaspoon nutmeg

Beat 1 egg, then add the rice and garlic. Spread the mixture in a greased 9-inch pie pan to form a crust. Chill thoroughly.

Cook the spinach in a saucepan until wilted, drain, and squeeze out all liquid. Melt the butter in a separate skillet, and sauté the leeks until tender, stirring occasionally. In a blender or medium bowl, combine the eggs, cheeses, cream, cayenne, and nutmeg. Blend well, then stir in the spinach and leeks. Pour the filling into the rice crust and bake at 350 degrees for 35 minutes, or until firm to the touch. Serve hot.

TEN

Salads

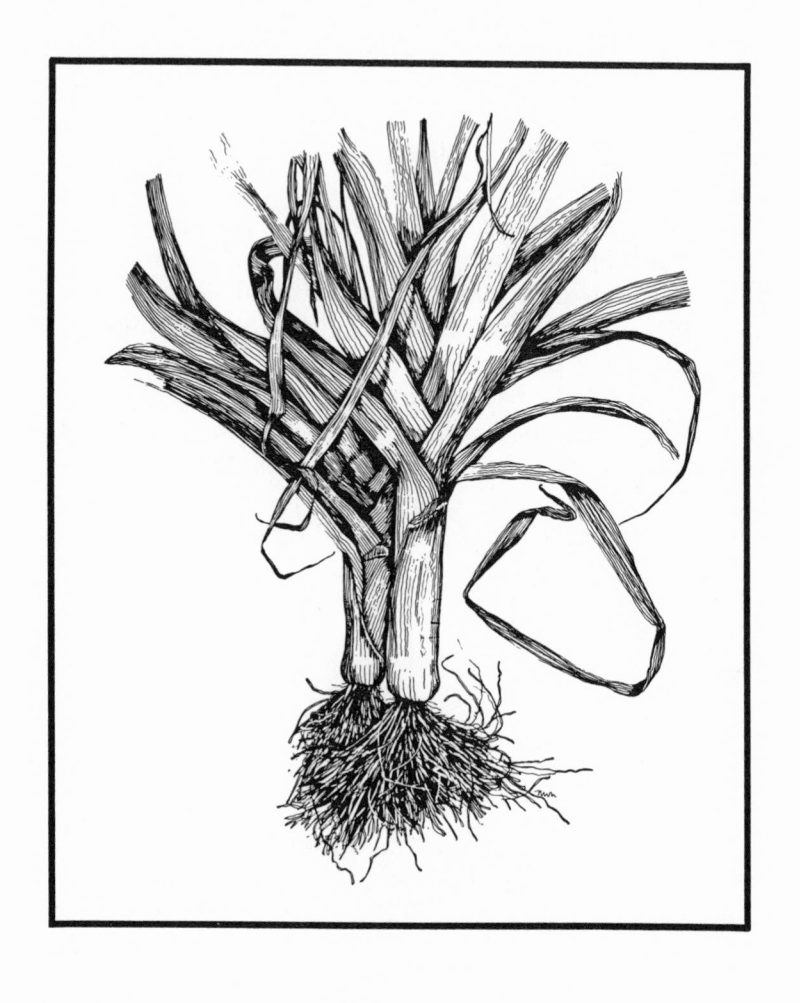

WHEN imagination is used in exploring the possibilities of preparing salads with leeks, the remarkable versatility of this vegetable becomes apparent. Taste combinations are nearly endless and can be subtle or surprising. What other vegetable tastes great with such diverse foods as tomatoes, grains, avocados, seafood, peppers, olives— even grapefruit?

Leeks have been used in green salads for hundreds of years: the recipe for Salat dates from about 1390. Today, their popularity in a wide variety of salads is growing. When used raw in leafy green salads, leeks are best minced or finely chopped. Marinating them in a little cider vinegar before adding to the other salad ingredients seems to bring out their natural sweetness. Leeks can replace the more mundane onions in potato or macaroni salads, fine as a light main course on a hot summer's day or as a salad course for a heartier meal. Tabouli, with the fresh, lively flavors of lemon, parsley, and mint, is especially good when made with leeks.

Leeks in salads may seem unusual at first, but with a little experimentation you will discover a wide variety of salads for everyday and special occasions. Ranging from the simple to the exotic, the following recipes offer a pleasant change from ordinary leafy greens that is welcome summer or winter.

Salat

From *The Forme of Cury*, compiled by the head cooks of King Richard II of England.

"Take parsel, sawge, garlec, chibollas [young onions], onyons, leek, borage, myntes, porrectes [a kind of leek], fenel, and ton tressis [cresses], rew, rosemarye, purslarye [purslane, a 'weed']; lave, and waisshe hem clene; pike hem, pluk hem small with thyn [thine] honde, and myng [mix] hem wel with raw oyle. Lay on vynegar and salt, and serve it forth."

SALADS

Leeks Vinaigrette

SERVES 6

6 medium leeks, of uniform size if possible
Vinaigrette Dressing (see page 115)
Chopped fresh herbs

Slice the leeks in half lengthwise, or cut into 3-inch rounds, and steam until barely tender. Drain. Transfer to a serving bowl and cover with the Vinaigrette Dressing while still warm. Marinate for at least 3 hours and serve chilled, garnished with chopped herbs.

VARIATIONS

Follow basic directions for Leeks Vinaigrette, combining the leeks with a variety of vegetables. For each recipe, steam the leeks and the other vegetables separately before arranging in serving bowl and marinating.

Leeks
Cooked white beans
Diced potatoes

Leeks
Chanterelle or button mushrooms
Fresh broad beans or baby limas
Diced or tiny new potatoes

Leeks
Jerusalem artichoke matchsticks
Hard boiled eggs
Diced celery (use uncooked)

Leeks
Carrot slices
Green beans

Leeks
Tomato wedges (use uncooked)
Artichoke hearts
Onion rings (use uncooked)

Sweet Peppers and Leeks   SERVES 4

3 sweet red peppers, halved and seeded
6 medium leeks, sliced in half lengthwise
Zesty French Dressing (see page 116)

Broil the peppers until the skin begins to blister; remove from heat. Steam and drain the leeks. Arrange the vegetables on a serving dish while still warm. Pour the dressing over the vegetables and chill thoroughly.

Leek and Shrimp Salad   SERVES 4

6 medium leeks, sliced in half lengthwise
2 cups cooked shrimp
1 large or 2 small heads tender Boston lettuce, torn into pieces
Basic French Dressing (see page 115)

Steam the leeks until tender, drain and chill. Place the lettuce on a serving dish, lay the leeks on top, and arrange the shrimp over the leeks. Spoon the dressing over all and chill.

Avocado and Leek Salad

6 small leeks
2 ripe avocados
Alfalfa sprouts
Walnut French Dressing (see page 116)

Poach the leeks whole in water or white wine. Drain and cool. Slice the avocados and arrange on the alfalfa sprouts with the leeks. If the salad is not to be served immediately, squeeze half a lemon over the avocado slices to preserve their color. Serve with chilled Walnut French Dressing.

Leek and Grapefruit Salad

An improbable but surprisingly good combination.

6 small leeks, whole, or 3 medium leeks, sliced in half
4 grapefruits, peeled and thinly sliced
Honey Fruit Dressing (see page 118) or Creamy French
      Dressing (see page 115)

Steam the leeks until they are bright green and tender. Arrange the grapefruit slices on a serving platter, place the leeks on top, and pour the dressing over all. Serve chilled.

Leekish Cole Slaw

1 small, solid head of cabbage
1 small leek, or green tops of 2, minced
1 carrot, grated
6 sprigs fresh parsley, minced
Tangy Yogurt Dressing (see page 117)

Grate the cabbage or shred very finely with a sharp knife. Combine with the leek, carrot, and parsley. Pour dressing over the vegetables, mix well and chill. Serve cold.

Lovely Layered Salad   SERVES 6 TO 8

Particularly beautiful when served in a glass bowl.

1 large or 2 small heads iceberg or Boston lettuce, torn into
    pieces
8 slices bacon, crisped and crumbled, or 1 can water chestnuts,
    drained and sliced
1 package frozen peas, separated
1 medium leek, cut in julienne strips
1 stalk celery, cut in julienne strips
½ cup chopped green pepper
1 to 2 cups grated sharp Cheddar cheese
Creamy Yogurt Dressing (see page 116)

Cover the bottom of a serving dish, preferably a clear glass one, with about half of the lettuce. Add a sprinkling of bacon or water chestnuts, then some of the peas. Add a layer of the remaining vegetables, then a layer of cheese, sprinkling more peas between each layer. Repeat, ending with cheese. Pour 1 cup Creamy Yogurt Dressing over the entire salad, cover, and refrigerate at least 3 hours before serving.

Salade Niçoise

SERVES 6

1 head lettuce, preferably Buttercrunch
1½ cups potatoes, cooked and cubed
½ to ¾ pound green beans, French-cut and cooked until
    tender
2 medium sized beets, cooked and diced
2 fresh tomatoes, cut in wedges
1 small leek, including some of green top, minced
3 hardboiled eggs, halved lengthwise
1 can anchovies or albacore, drained
Vinaigrette Dressing, substituting red wine vinegar (see page
    115)

Wash, separate, and dry the lettuce and lay in the bottom of a glass serving bowl or shallow glass dish. Prepare the vegetables and arrange over the lettuce in mounds like wedges of pie, using the minced leek to deliniate "slices." Garnish with hardboiled eggs and anchovies or albacore. Spoon Vinaigrette Dressing over all and chill. Toss salad at the table just before serving.

Leek and Yogurt Salad

SERVES 6

2 medium leeks, sliced lengthwise or in thick rounds
1 cup plain yogurt
2 tablespoons lemon juice
2 tablespoons minced parsley
1 teaspoon dill or mint
Salt and pepper to taste

Steam the leeks until bright green and barely tender. Drain. Combine the remaining ingredients, and pour over the leeks while they are still warm. Chill for at least 1 hour. Serve cold.

Macaroni Salad with Leeks   SERVES 6

2 cups whole wheat macaroni
1 cup cottage cheese
2 teaspoons Dijon mustard
1 small leek, chopped fine
2 fresh tomatoes, chopped fine
1 cup fresh peas
3 tablespoons chopped fresh parsley
Salt and pepper to taste

Cook the macaroni in 2 quarts boiling water until tender, drain well, and chill. Whirl the cottage cheese smooth in a blender. Mix with the macaroni, add remaining ingredients, and chill at least 30 minutes before serving.

Hot Leek and Potato Salad   SERVES 6

6 large potatoes
3 tablespoons oil
3 tablespoons white wine vinegar
1 small jar marinated artichoke hearts
2 small leeks, minced
2 stalks celery, chopped
1 teaspoon dry mustard
Salt and pepper to taste
6 hardboiled eggs, chopped
2 tablespoons parsley, minced

Boil the potatoes until tender. Measure the oil and vinegar into a large bowl and add the artichoke hearts, leeks, celery, mustard, salt and pepper. Toss together gently and allow to marinate. Peel the cooked potatoes, then cube and combine with the other ingredients. Add the eggs and parsley, mixing well. Place in a 350-degree oven for about 10 minutes to heat through.

Tabouli Leeky

1½ to 2 cups raw bulgar (cracked wheat)
3 cups water or stock
¾ cup cooked white beans
3 medium tomatoes, chopped
1 small leek, including green top, minced
½ cup chopped parsley
1 to 4 tablespoons minced fresh mint
3 tablespoons olive oil
Juice of 2 lemons
1 clove garlic, minced
Salt and pepper to taste
Romaine lettuce leaves

Bring the bulgar and water or stock to a boil, turn off heat, and let stand, covered, for 1 hour. Drain. Add the remaining ingredients except the lettuce, toss well, and chill. Serve on the lettuce leaves.

Tomato and Leek Aspic

1¾ cups tomato or vegetable juice
1 envelope unflavored gelatin, or ¾ stick agar agar
2 tablespoons lemon juice or cider vinegar
Dash of Worcestershire sauce
1 small leek, or green tops of 2, minced
1 teaspoon honey
Bibb lettuce
Mayonnaise

Soak gelatin or agar agar in tomato or vegetable juice for 15 minutes, then simmer until dissolved. Add the remaining ingredients and mix thoroughly. Pour into individual molds and chill until set. Unmold and serve on a bed of Bibb lettuce, garnished with mayonnaise.

VARIATIONS

Tomato and Leek Aspic with Shrimp

Follow the basic recipe above, but fold in 1 cup cooked, cleaned shrimp when salad is partially set.

Tomato and Leek Aspic with Cottage Cheese

Follow the basic recipe, adding 1 cup cottage cheese before pouring into molds.

Avocado and Leek Mold   SERVES 4

2 cups beef or vegetable stock (or bouillon)
1 package unflavored gelatin
Juice of 1 lemon
1 ripe avocado, sliced very thin
3 medium leeks, sliced thin
Salad greens

Bring the stock to a boil and pour over the gelatin. Stir until dissolved. Add the lemon juice, and pour half of the liquid into a 2-quart mold. Add avocado slices, mixing gently. Chill until the consistency of unbeaten egg whites.
Steam and drain leeks. Add to the remaining stock and pour the mixture into the mold. Refrigerate overnight. Unmold on a bed of greens, and serve with Zesty French Dressing (see page 116) or Tangy Yogurt Dressing with lemon juice (see page 117).

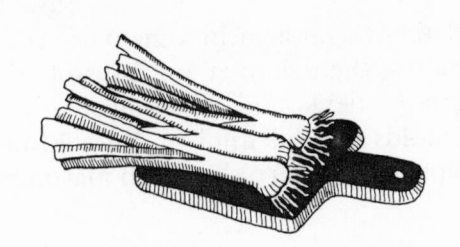

Jellied Borscht with Leeks   SERVES 4

Ruby red and sparkling, this salad is beautiful as well as tasty.

2 small leeks, sliced thin
¾ cup grated raw beets
¼ cup minced celery
1 cup beef or vegetable stock (or bouillon)
1 cup water
1 envelope unflavored gelatin
1 tablespoon grated onion
2 tablespoons lemon juice
½ teaspoon honey (optional)
Alfalfa sprouts or mixed salad greens

Simmer the leeks, beets, and celery in stock for 10 minutes, or until just tender. Soften the gelatin in water. Combine with the vegetable mixture, and stir until gelatin is dissolved. Add the onion, lemon juice, and honey and mix thoroughly. Pour into a mold, and chill until set. Unmold on sprouts or salad greens. This can be served plain or with Tangy Yogurt Dressing (see page 117).

Mock Salmon Mousse   SERVES 6

1 envelope unflavored gelatin
¾ cup cold water
2 cups tomato purée
1 3-ounce package cream cheese
¾ cup mayonnaise
Salt and pepper to taste
1 medium leek, chopped fine
1 cup chopped celery
½ cup chopped green pepper
1 package frozen peas, separated
1 can flaked tuna or crab meat
Salad greens

Dissolve the gelatin in ¼ cup of the water. Heat the remaining water with tomato purée to boiling and stir in gelatin. Continue stirring until gelatin has melted. Add the cream cheese and mayonnaise to the hot tomato mixture, blend well, and season to taste. Allow to cool while you prepare the vegetables, then stir in vegetables and the flaked tuna or crab. Pour into a fish-shaped mold and chill until set. Unmold on a bed of greens.

Carolyn's Molded Seafood Salad Supreme
SERVES 8 TO 10

2 cups crushed whole wheat crackers
6 hardboiled eggs, finely chopped
1 can crab, drained
1 can shrimp, drained
1 cup grated white Cheddar cheese
1 small green pepper, chopped
1 2-ounce jar pimientos, drained
3 small leeks, including green tops, finely chopped
Mayonnaise to hold
Bibb lettuce

Combine all the ingredients and pack into a 2-quart mold. Chill overnight. Unmold onto tender Bibb lettuce leaves, or serve as a paté with crackers.

DRESSINGS

Vinaigrette Dressing   MAKES 1 CUP

½ cup olive oil
¼ cup lemon juice or wine vinegar
2 tablespoons water
1 teaspoon minced fresh chives
1 teaspoon minced fresh parsley
1 teaspoon minced fresh tarragon
1 large clove garlic, minced or pressed
Salt and pepper to taste

Combine all the ingredients and pour over warm, steamed vegetables to marinate.

Basic French Dressing   MAKES 1 CUP

⅔ cup olive oil
¼ cup lemon juice or wine vinegar
1 tablespoon water
Salt and pepper
½ teaspoon honey

Combine all the ingredients in a blender or a jar with a tight-fitting lid, and blend or shake until well mixed.

VARIATIONS

Creamy French Dressing   MAKES 1 CUP

Follow directions for Basic French, adding:

2 teaspoons paprika
1 egg
pinch of cayenne pepper

Zesty French Dressing   MAKES 1 CUP

Follow directions for Basic French, adding:

1 tablespoon Dijon mustard
1 large clove garlic, pressed
½ teaspoon cracked pepper
¼ teaspoon dried parsley
¼ teaspoon dried thyme
½ teaspoon dried oregano

Walnut French Dressing   MAKES 1 CUP

Follow directions for Basic French, adding:

1 small clove garlic, pressed
2 tablespoons finely chopped walnuts

Creamy Yogurt Dressing   MAKES 1 CUP

½ cup plain yogurt
½ cup mayonnaise
1 tablespoon honey
Salt and pepper to taste

Combine all the ingredients thoroughly. The honey is
needed to liquefy the dressing.

Tangy Yogurt Dressing

MAKES 1 CUP

¾ cup plain yogurt
2 tablespoons mayonnaise
3 tablespoons lemon juice or tarragon vinegar
½ teaspoon dry mustard
1 teaspoon honey
1 teaspoon celery seed or fennel seed
1 clove garlic, minced
Salt and pepper to taste

Combine all the ingredients thoroughly.

VARIATION

Dilly Yogurt Dressing

MAKES 1 CUP

Follow directions for Tangy Yogurt Dressing, omitting celery or fennel seed, and adding:

2 tablespoons minced parsley
1 teaspoon fresh dill

Whirl the ingredients in blender until the herbs are finely chopped.

Horseradish Yogurt Dressing

MAKES 1 CUP

¾ cup plain yogurt
2 tablespoons mayonnaise
1 tablespoon horseradish (more or less, to taste)
1 tablespoon minced leek

Combine all the ingredients.

Green Goddess Dressing

MAKES 1½ CUPS

½ cup plain yogurt
½ cup sour cream
½ cup mayonnaise
3 tablespoons tarragon vinegar
3 tablespoons cider vinegar
1 large clove garlic, pressed
1 generous tablespoon anchovy paste (optional)
⅓ cup fresh parsley
2 to 3 tablespoons coarsely chopped leek

Whirl all the ingredients in a blender until smooth and delicately green in color.

Honey Fruit Salad Dressing

MAKES 2 CUPS

½ cup honey, warmed to liquefy
1 teaspoon dry mustard
3 tablespoons lemon juice
3 tablespoons cider vinegar
Salt to taste
1 cup oil
2 teaspoons finely minced leek
1 to 2 teaspoons celery, fennel or poppy seeds

Combine the honey, dry mustard, lemon juice, vinegar, and salt. Add the oil, drop by drop at first and then in a thin stream, beating constantly—an electric mixer or blender makes this easy. Stir in the minced leek and seeds. Tightly covered, this dressing will keep for weeks.

Index